Seer

Visions Dreams & Prophecy
Isle of Skye & The Hebrides

Steve Taylor

Shennachie Press

SEER

Visions Dreans & Prophecy
Isle of Skye & The Hebrides

Copyright © 2023 Steve Taylor

ISBN: 978-1-4478-3399-4

First published 2023

Shennachie Press

In Memory

of

Norman MacLeod
An T-Ob
Isle Of Harris

1926 - 2006

Gentleman
Friend
Seer

Contents

CHAPTER 1

Introduction

The subject commonly called the Second Sight I think might be more fitly called the First Sight, because it for the most part sees things before they are.

Andrew Simson (c1707)

The subject of what has been called 'Second Sight', 'Prophecy' or 'Foreknowledge', has fascinated and terrified people in equal measure for thousands of years. From the finger writing on a wall revealing the fate of the Babylonian monarch Belshazzar, whose face 'turned pale', in 539 B.C., to the subsequently alarmed and despairing citizen on the Isle of Eigg on Scotland's west coast in 1690, who, ignoring the warnings of a local Seer, suffered at the hands of hostile forces, people have both listened to, laughed, mocked and scorned the words and warnings of the Prophet.

In religious circles, the same is true, as both Scottish Protestant and Roman Catholic clergy appear to have been, as they still are, divided over the issue. Some see these gifts as legitimate while others regard them as having questionable origins and have sought, as we will see, to discourage or expunge them completely. And this question of 'origin'[1] is one that, for many, has never been fully or satisfactorily addressed. As a result, some seek to sweep the issue under the carpet or plunge their heads into the sand. Others call for outright condemnation and seek, by all means, to discredit the gift. However, even the most ardent cynic cannot explain how the gift they oppose or deny so strongly has manifested itself so profoundly and is even to be found among those they themselves regard as people of high standing, unimpeachable honesty and orthodoxy.

It was to try and clarify issues such as these once and for all that men like Rev. John Fraser (c1647-c1702) wrote his book *Deuteroscopia*, published posthumously in 1707, by Andrew Simson the husband of his niece.[2] Fraser was born in Mull, son of the minister of Tiree and Coll. Educated at Glasgow University he returned to his home area as chaplain to Sir Allan MacLean, prior to succeeding his father as minister of Tiree and Coll and Dean of the Isles. A similar but much larger and more widely researched book on the same subject entitled - *A Treatise on the Second Sight,* dated 1763, was written by a Skye resident under the pseudonym 'Theophilus Insulanus'.[3] Both these books sought to prove the veracity and validity of the gift and experience as well as dealing with the many objections to it. What is amazing is that the vast majority of Skye ministers who were asked to contribute material to Theophilus Insulanus's book were sympathetic to the subject.[4]

Of course, not all island ministers were so inclined:

> Under date Tuesday, Sept. 7, 1773, when Johnson and Boswell were at Corrichatachin, in the Broadford district of Skye, Boswell writes - "Johnson inquired here, if there were any remains of the Second-Sight. Mr Macpherson, minister of Slate, said, he was resolved not to believe it, because it was founded on no principle."[5]

In addition to Theophilus Insulanus and Fraser, we have other independent evidence from writers of their era, such as Martin Martin (Màrtainn MacGilleMhàrtainn c.1660-1718) in his 1702 publication - *A Description of the Western Islands of Scotland.*[6]

While all but the most blinkered would admit to the reality of the experiences related in the books referred to, most of which are drawn from Skye, Lewis/Harris and other Hebridean islands, sceptics and naysayers remained. Among the critics, there were also those of a more scientific bent and others who found it hard to hide their contempt for the people of the Islands and Highlands. One such was E. A. F. Browne, Psychological Consultant at the Crighton Instition, Dumfries. He addressed such phenomena and the people who experienced it in an article *Second Sight or Deuteroscopia,* in *The Journey of Psychological Medicine,* in May 1786:

> The localisation (of Second Sight) in this country has been limited to the Highlands and Islands and to the Celtic race, even to Skye and the vexed Hebrides, where the burst-boom of the mighty Atlantic echoes and expends itself amongst the gigantic cliffs which wall in thee semi-sterile hills, or morasses; where the shepherd, his flocks - mayhap the hardy deer - secure drowsily and slowly scanty nourishment; where mists, and exhalations, and long - continued twilight favour visual deceptions; and where a people that have passed recently and rapidly from Paganism to Catholicism and to Protestantism, to Christianity without its twin civilisation, and are by constitution gloomy, dreamy, and uneducated, are prone to superstition, to create and to credit imaginary communications and warnings from the world of spirits.

Of course, the books we have been referring to and the experiences they relate to took place before evangelical Christianity had arrived in these islands. This did not happen until the early part of the nineteenth century. And yet, when it did, instead of being the death knell for the supernatural, there was a resurgence of a deep, mysterious, unpredictable, spirituality where the gift and its experience was renewed and transformed into something that could clearly, for some at any rate, now be recognised as, 'of God'. The term used to describe the gift of second sight, foreknowledge or revelation would, within the evangelical community here in the Highlands and Islands, become known as 'the secret of the Lord'. However, the issue for some, even those who experienced such things personally, (as we will see later) would remain to be the thorny issue of 'source'.

Interestingly, the first Christian Missionary ever to visit Skye, the Irish Abbot and Evangelist Columba or Colmcille (521-597) is recorded as speaking prophetically during his first visit to the island. Montalembert, in his *Life of St Columba*, gives an account of this incident:

> One day while Columba was labouring in his evangelical work in Skye, he cried out all at once, "My sons, to-day you will see an ancient Pictish chief, who has kept faithfully all his life the precepts of the natural law, arrive in this island; he comes to be baptised and to die." Immediately after a boat was seen to approach the shore with a feeble old man seated in the prow, who was recognised as the chief of one of the neighbouring tribes. Two of his companions took him up in their arms and brought him before the missionary, to whose words, as repeated by the interpreter, he listened attentively. When the discourse was ended the old man asked to be baptised, and immediately after breathed his last breath, and was buried in the very spot where he had just been brought to shore.[7]

Another issue which, at times, causes some confusion in this realm is terminology. The title used of someone with the ability to foretell the future is usually that of 'Seer' or 'Prophet'. Although used much more rarely the title 'soothsayer' or 'prognosticator' were, in the past, also used. In religious circles today the term used of those who claim or practice this gift is almost exclusively 'Prophet', while in the past it was 'Seer'.[8]

At the same time we have various starting points for any given revelation - such as having its source in a 'vision', 'dream', 'premonition', 'impression' and so forth. Furthermore, there is a language of more recent vintage, which we find used in some religious circles today, particularly within the Charismatic movement, where terms such as 'words of knowledge' or a 'word from the Lord', are employed. While by no means discounting these, the abuse of them, particularly within this movement in the USA, has brought it into much disrepute.

But it is not the present we are addressing in this current book – but the past, where, both within religious communities and outside them, the words and predictions of the 'Seer' or 'Prophet' are so well attested. What follows is also a unique glimpse in to a past generation in Skye and its sister islands. Consequently, we will not always be rushing to the points of our considerations without setting them in the context of the peoples and communities in which they took place.

From the time when the seaboard of northwest Scotland was ruled by the Norse (c 800-1263) and thereafter by the Lordship of the Isles (c1330-1493) and for some time thereafter this area was, for various reasons, a thorn in the flesh of the powers that be. And of course, playing in to the timeframe covered by this book, was, as we shall see, the recent Jacobite risings of 1689 and 1745 as well as other matters of political and military intrigue.

ENDNOTES

1. By 'origin' we mean whether or not the gift of foreknowledge has its source in the realms of darkness or the realms of light and involves either good or evil spirits or angels or in some other innocuous source.

Following on from the great evangelical movements which swept through these islands between the early 1800s right up until the mid 1950s, which both formed and influences Hebridean evangelicalism down to this day, the gift of the seer or prophet, if not outrightly condemned, as is has been to a great extent in more recent times, has only been recognised or tolerated as it is expressed within the confines and restrictions of the tradition. Anyone claiming or expressing the prophetic gift outside 'church' circles is viewed with, at least, extreme scepticism and the source of such revelation or experience as likely coming from the forces of spiritual darkness.

However, this view runs contrary to that of people like Fraser (who was by no means alone), who saw the gift as being much more widespread and available to people both outside and inside traditional religious communities. Such a view does not restrict The Eternal Spirit to the confines of any theology or otherwise - but recognises His freedom to reveal the future in dreams, vision, foreknowledge and prophesy to anyone at any time and in any place. Such a view, I believe, fits the facts much better than the restrictive conditions of many evangelical/charismatic churches today. It also gives a much wider gamut of 'source' - the issue that has concerned so many within 'church' circles.

2. Andrew Simson (later spelt Simpson) the posthumous publisher of the work, was connected to Fraser. He had married his niece, the only daughter of his brother Mathias Symson, Minister of Stirling, who died in 1664. Symson himself had been educated at Edinburgh, graduating in 1661, and was minister at Kirkinner from 1663 to 1686 and at Douglas from 1686 to 1869, prior to going to Edinburgh and setting up as a bookseller and printer. See - Michael Hunter, The Occult Laboratory, Magic, Science and Second Sight in Late Seventeenth-Century Scotland, (Boydell & Brewer, Boydell Press) 2001, p. 47.

3. The first edition of this book published in 1763 is titled - A Treatise On The Second Sight, Dreams and Apparitions: With Several Instances Sufficiently Attested; And An Appendix Of Others Equally Authentic: The Whole Illustrated With Letters To And From The Author On The Subject of his Treatise; And A Short Dissertation on the Mischievous Effects of Loose Principles - by Theophilus Insulanus. Booksellers, reprints of the original and   Library's identify 'Theophilus Insulanus' as a   pseudonym for 'Donald MacLeod'. The 1819 edition is attributed to - 'Theophilus Insulanus (Rev. Donald MacLeod, William MacLeod, of Hamer in Skye (M'Leod of Hamir), as well as 'Rev. Mr. Frazer, Mr. Martin, John Aubrey, Esq F. R. S.'

In The Great Book of Skye, Skye, historians Prof. Norman MacDonald and Cailean Maclean identify the author of the original book published in 1763 as William MacLeod of Hamer (Glendale), Skye (GBOS 1 - p.355).

In the book - *History of the MacLeods with genealogies of the principal families of the name,* published in 1889, we find the following noted in relation to William MacLeod of Hammer - ' William MacLeod, who, in 1763, published a curious treatise on " Second Sight," under the nom de plume of "Theophilus Insulanus." (p.262.)

In a recent (2023) summary of the book, a knowledgeable seller notes in part - 'The identity of Theophilus Insulanus remains a mystery. Originally thought to be the Reverend Donald McLeod of Hamer (or Hammair), Skye, a recent work in 2020 suggests that a William McLeod was our 'friend of God on the Island' as his Greco-Latin pseudonym translates to.'

However, from some of the stories told by the author of this book it would appear that the writer was a minister - or at least a person to whom people turned for spiritual advice, councel and comfort. The only problem with this assumption is that there is no record of a Skye minister called Donald MacLeod fitting the required profile during this time period - at least as far as the author can establish.

In 1754 a Rev. Donald MacLeod was inducted as minister to Durinish, Skye. He was born about 1698. *Fasti* records of him (pp.,168-169) - 'The son of Norman M.of Grishernish and great-grandson of Sir Rory Mor M. of Dunvegan; educated at King's College, Aberdeen; M.A. (9th April 1718); was missionary in Benbecula; ord. to South Uist 8th Oct. 1725; trans, to North Uist 4th May 1736; called 2nd Jan., trans, and adm. 13th Aug. 1754; died after having been warned by a notable woman seer 27th Dec. 1759.' Theophilus Insulanus refers to this man in his book.

Fasti Ecclesiae Scoticanae: the succession of ministers in the Church of Scotland from the reformation, records a Rev. William MacLeod, presented by George II to Barra in 1742 and transferred to Bracadale, Skye on the 4th of May 1749. This man left Skye in 1767 to become a Minister in Campbeltown, Kintyre.

4. Another book of interest from this era is Robert Kirk's *The Secret Commonwealth.* Robert Kirk (1644-1692) was a minister, Gaelic scholar and folklorist. *The Secret Commonwealth* is a collection of folklore collected between 1691-1692 and published in 1815.

5. Quoted in - Norman MacRae, *Highland second-sight, with prophecies of Coinneach Odhar and the Seer of Petty, and numerous other examples from the writings of Aubrey, Martin, Theophilus Insulanus, the Rev. John Fraser, dean of Argyle and the Isles, Rev. Dr. Kennedy of Dingwall, and others.* (George Souter, Dingwall.) 1909 p.82.

6. Martin was a native of Bealach, near Duntulm on Skye. He was born around 1660. He was a son of Donald Martin, who served with the MacDonalds of Sleat under James Graham, 1st Marquess of Montrose, and his wife Màiri, who was a niece of Dòmhnall Gorm Òg MacDonald, 1st Baronet of Sleat. He is thought to have had at least two brothers, one of whom may have been tacksman at Flodigarry on Skye.

Martin graduated with an MA from the University of Edinburgh, in 1681. Between 1681 and 1686, he was a tutor to Dòmhnall a' Chogaidh, 4th Baronet of Sleat, and, from 1686 to 1695, he was tutor and governor to Ruaraidh Òg MacLeod of Harris. Much of this period was spent in Edinburgh where the young chief was a student at the university

Martin undertook his voyage to St. Kilda in May 1697 and his tour of Lewis in 1699 under the patronage of Hans Sloane, the Secretary of the Royal Society in London. The Scottish antiquary, Sir Robert Sibbald, considered that his command of Gaelic, knowledge of the customs of Gaeldom and connections with Hebridean elites made him well qualified for the task. He was an assiduous collector of natural specimens and minerals during his trips.

Both Samuel Johnson and Boswell read his book and took a copy of it along with them on their famous tour in 1773. Johnson felt Martin had failed to record the more interesting aspects of life at the time, and suggested that this was because he was unaware of just how different the social structure of the Western Isles was in comparison to life elsewhere. Some of Martin's descriptions of second sight and other superstitions led Johnson to regard him as credulous. (Wikipedia)

7. Quoted in - Alexander Cameron, *The History and Traditions of the Isle of Skye,* (E. Forsyth, Bank Street, Inverness, 1871) p.9. See also - http://www. strobertbellarmine.net/books/Montalembert--Columba.pdf

8. We are not addressing here the practice of divination, sorcery, fortunetelling, witchcraft, casting spells, holding séances, or channelling with the dead (Necromancy), all of which appear to be prohibited in the Jewish scriptures (Deuteronomy 18:10-12) and would have, I surmise, been frowned upon by most of the people we are examining here. However, that is not to say that such practices do not result in true communication with the world of the spirits, such as was the case when a woman identified as 'a witch of Endor' consulted with the dead prophet Samuel as recorded in the Jewish Torah (1 Samuel 28:10-12). Historian Douglas Ansdell has noted: 'When Donald MacQueen was appointed minister of Kilmuir (Skye) in 1740, the belief in witchcraft was very common in so much that he had many prosecutions before his session.' However, we are left

in the dark as to any detail, begging the question; were those prosecuted simply people who believed in and experienced the supernatural - as well as perhaps using the natural remedies which were so common throughout the culture of the Highlands and Islands?

CHAPTER 2

Seers & Dreamers

This unusual vision did much expose the Seer, for all the inhabitants treated him as a fool, though he had on several other occasions foretold things that afterwards were accomplished.

Martin Martin (c1703)

In the year 1685 there lived, in the township of Kildonan, Isle of Eigg a man, identified only as a 'Tenant' and supporter of 'Clan Rannold'. Of him it is recorded that he,

> Told publickly to the whole Inhabitants upon the Lord's day after Divine service, performed by Father O Rain, then Priest of that place. That they should all flit out of that Isle, and plant themselves some where else; Because that People of strange and different habits and Arms, were to come to the Isle and to use all acts of Hostility, as Killing, Burning, Tirling and Deforceing of Women; Finally to discharge all that the hands of an Enemy could do; but what they were, or whence they came, he could not tell.

The population seems, for the most part, to have ignored the warning. However, over the intervening weeks and months, the man persisted and pled with the people to heed his warning to leave. As a result, it is said, several families moved and settled on the nearby Isle of Canna.

What this Seer certainly had no way of knowing was that a Major James Ferguson[1] would, some time thereafter, be placed in command of a detachment of some 600 troops charged with subduing the Western Isles, nor that he would sail towards them from Greenock in May 1690. The captain of the ship on which the troops would travel was one Edward Pottinger.

In June of 1689, the Seer fell sick and 'Father O Rain'[2] was sent for 'in order to give him the benefit of Absolution and Extreme Unction'. A number of other people accompanied the priest to visit the dying man, some of whom tried to persuade him of the folly of his previous prediction and pled with him to recant. However, he informed them that they would soon discover the truth of what he had predicted. He died a short time later.

An eyewitness to what followed on the Island of Eigg was the aforementioned Rev. John Frazer. He takes up his own story:

> Within fourteen or fifteen days thereafter (of the death of the Seer), I was Eye witness (being then Prisoner with Captain Pottinger) to the truth of what he did foretell, and being before hand well instructed of all that he said, I did admire to see it particularly verified; especially, that of the different habits and Arms, some being clad with Red coats, some with White Coats, and Granadier Capes, some Armed with Sword and Pike, and some with Sword and Musket.

It is almost certain that what follows relates to the same Seer of Eigg – even although he is not specifically identified. However, be that the case or not it is certainly further proof of the veracity of

11

his prediction. The following is recorded by Martin Martin in his classic book: *A Description of the Western Islands of Scotland* (1703).

One who had been accustomed to see the Second Sight, in the isle of Egg, which lies about three or four leagues to the south-west part of the isle of Sky, told his neighbours that he had frequently seen an apparition of a man in a red coat lined with blue, and having on his head a strange sort of blue cap, with a very high cock on the fore-part of it, and that the man who there appeared, was kissing a comely maid in the village where the Seer dwelt; and therefore declared that a man in such a dress would certainly debauch or marry such a young woman. This unusual vision did much expose the Seer, for all the inhabitants treated him as a fool, though he had on several other occasions foretold things that afterwards were accomplished; this they thought one of the most unlikely things to be accomplished, that could have entered into any man's head. This story was then discoursed of in the isle of Sky, and all that heard it, laughed at it; it being a rarity to see any foreigner in Egg, and the young woman had no thoughts of going any where else. This story was told me at Edinburgh, by Normand MacLeod of Graban, in September 1688, he being just then come from the isle of Sky; and there were present, the laird of MacLeod, and Mr. Alexander MacLeod, Advocate, and others. About a year and a half after the late revolution, Major Ferguson, now Colonel of one of her majesty's regiments of foot, was then sent by the government with six hundred men, and some frigates to reduce the islanders that had appeared for K. J. (King James) and perhaps the small isle of Egg had never been regarded, though some of the inhabitants had been at the battle of Killicranky,[3] but by a mere socident, which determined Major Ferguson to go to the isle of Egg, which was this: a boat's crew of the isle of Egg, happened to be in the isle of Sky, and killed one of Major Ferguson's soldiers there; upon notice of which, the Major directed his course to the isle of Egg, where he was sufficiently revenged of the natives: and at the same time, the maid above mentioned being very handsome, was then forcibly carried on board one of the vessels, by some of the soldiers, where she was kept above twenty-four hours, and ravished, and brutishly robbed at the same time of her fine head of hair: she is since married in the isle, and in good reputation; her misfortune being pitied, and not reckoned her crime.

One of the most common experiences of Second Sight is in connection with portents surrounding death. This is true in all of the literature which records such phenomenon as well as in personal instances known to the author. These are far too numerous to mention in detail - but a number are recorded as they relate historically to Skye and the Hebrides. These come from the pen of 'Theophilus Insulanus'.

> One Thursday morning, in October 1751, Archibald MacQueen, son of the Rev Archibald MacQueen, minister of Snizort, Skye, walked out of the farmhouse in Glenhaultin which was the family home, intending to walk some 6 miles through the hills to Rigg, on Skye's east coast, to visit a friend. However, about four o'clock in the afternoon and within a very short distance of his intended destination he took a seizure and fell to the ground. The man he was about to visit, a Mr. Nicolson, who was a physician, saw him fall and rushed to help - but he was already dead.

Due to the late hour, fading light and distance it was not possible to send word of the tragic news to his family in Glenaultin that day. So it was that his parents went to bed that night unaware of the tragic death of their son. However between 11 pm and midnight, 'they heard a lamentable noise about the house, as it were women mourning; whereupon Mr. Archibald ordered people immediately to look out what the matter was, but they saw nothing, so went to bed.' No sooner had they returned to bed than they heard, 'the same lamentation and clapping of hands, which is a Highland custom with women to express their grief for the loss of near friends.' Again, MacQueen, had someone check outside - but again nothing was seen. Some 20 minutes later the same sound was heard yet again. This time Mrs MacQueen and her sister left the house together, searching the grounds, but yet again nothing was found. Archibald MacQueen senior was 'a weak tender old man, about eighty years of age' at this time and both he and the others in the house did not sleep for the remainder of the night. About 8 am the following morning a messenger arrived with the tragic news 'whereupon the whole family were in an uproar of cries and lamentation.'

Interestingly the above story was related to 'Allan MacDonald, younger of Kingsborough' (1720-1792), by 'Mr. Archibald's wife and servant.' Allan MacDonald was of course the husband of Flora MacDonald, forever linked and made famous for her part in helping Bonnie Prince Charlie escape from the Isle of South Uist to Skye, thus evading the English armed forces who were doing their utmost to try and capture him.

Allan MacDonald appears to have had more than a passing interest in this subject as he wrote an extensive letter, dated 22nd December 1756, to Theophilus Insulanus on the subject.

On rare occasions, it appears that visions or dreams of future events are given to more than one person at the same time. Both of the following instances were again supplied by Allan MacDonald:

> In the end of the year 1744, fourteen persons saw a large vessel coming in below Kingsborough, in the dusk of the evening, and drop anchor in the entrance of Loch Snizort, a very uncommon harbour, which surprised us all. This sight we had till night deprived us of it; but next morning there was no vessel to be found, so that we all agreed it to be the Second Sight, which was soon accomplished; for Captain Ferguson being in search of the young Pretender (Bonnie Prince Charlie), with the Furnace sloop of war, anchored exactly in the dusk of the evening, in that unusual place above-mentioned, half a mile below the house of Kingsborough.

Little did Allan MacDonald know at the time, nor could he possibly have imagined, that some two years after seeing this vision of the 'Furnace' the very same vessel would spirit his future wife from Skye to an uncertain fate in London, nor that Ferguson would also be responsible for the arrest of his father and his subsequent incarceration in Edinburgh.

But back to Allan MacDonald's second story:

> Alexander MacDonald, alias MacRanald, (a person of known courage and honour) coming from Slate to my father's house, in the year 1747, we accidentally fell upon the subject of the Second Sight, which induced him to give us the following account. About five o'clock at night, he and half a dozen more, all honest tenants, came into the change-house of Kilmore in Slate, about a pistol-shot from the kirk, to take a moderate refreshment, it being in the month of December, then cold frosty weather. About an hour after coming in, he accidentally went to the door, which fronted the kirk-yard, saw, to his great surprise, the whole kirk-yard was covered over with men. Not only so, but heard the confused murmur of their speech, yet not so as to distinguish word by word, or to understand any part thereof; the moon was so bright, that he discerned a crowd about the place of burial distinctly, belonging to the family of MacDonald, and the rest of the company dispersed in twos and threes over the whole churchyard. After he had sufficiently satisfied his curiosity, he went in to the change-house, and told the company what he had seen, who immediately sprang to the door, and had the same sight for the space of ten minutes, and then it gradually vanished from their sight, they being ten in number. The wife of the house, her daughter and servant, are still in life, who were of the number that saw this vision; and, it is observable, that a month thereafter, the old Lady MacDonald was buried in the very spot where they imagined to have seen the throng of the people.

Alan MacDonald finished his series of accounts with the following story:

> For two years together, none of the Mistress of Garafad's (Garafad is in the Staffin area of northeast Skye) women would stay in her kiln, because of a corpse in its linens they frequently saw on the kiln-grish, or where corn is dried, a very unusual place indeed to lay corpses. But it happened, last year, that one MacPhail from Gearlough (Gairloch), with his whole crew, except one, were lost near Garafad; one of the corpses being found that evening, was carried on a bier, and left in the kiln on the drying-place; as the whole people expected to get the rest of the bodies immediately, they did not wait to go to a house with the one they had found ; and, so that corpse remained in the kiln all night; which every body remarked as the fulfilling of the Second Sight, which had been seen in the kiln before.

Another correspondent who replied to Theophilus Insulanus's request for information on the subject was 'Donald Martin of Beallach in Trotternish', Skye. He recorded the following story:

> Upon the first of January, 1733, three boys were late at night travelling together from the north of Duntulm, to the place of my residence at Beallach; the weakest of them, a boy of twelve years of age, walked a musket-shot behind the rest, and gave such a terrible cry, as alarmed his comrades much; upon their asking him what the matter was; he answered, that he was surrounded with some hundreds of men, and was surprised they did not see them likewise; upon which they told him there was no such thing, otherwise one of them would see the same; when he, with difficulty, (as he alleged,) came up to his comrades, he pointed out a certain spot, and told them there was a gentleman riding on a white horse before the crowd; then he cried out, that another rider had fallen from his horse, in a place hard by them: in short he confounded the other boys, pointing at the different sorts of people about him: they came to the

house and told me, and others still living, how much the boy surprised them, by what he alleged to have seen: I called him before the company, and asked him what was the matter; he told me every word as above. However, no notice was taken of it until the month of December thereafter. That the tutor of MacDonald's lady died, and there were a great number of people at the interment, so that the usual road was too narrow for them; the tutor ordered them to go on that road on which the boys had been travelling the preceding January. Upon this, what the boy had told occurred to me, being in company, and was resolved to take notice if any was to fall from his horse, in that place pointed out by the boy: the tutor's horse coming up to that very place, sunk in a bog, that some of the people brought him out of his saddle, for safety; and Donald Nicholson, late tacksman of Talmtean, was riding on a white horse before them all.

Theophilus Insulanus goes on in his book to relate a number of other stories in connection with our subject. One is in connection with a woman called Christian MacCaskill. He writes of her:

Despairing to recover of a long sickness, begged I should come to see her; with which having complied, and finding by visible symptom, she could not draw much time; after I had put her in mind of her approaching end, enquired if she saw the Second Sight, (as was commonly believed,) she answered, very oft, but not with any satisfaction. I then asked what age she might be of the first time she arrived at that knowledge? She answered seventeen years or thereby; and that then coming, in the dusk of the evening, to a tenant's house in Borradale, and sitting by the fire-side she saw one Kenneth Macaskil, who lived at a little distance, having a sheep belonging to herself, (which she had seen that day,) bound on the other side of the fire, and a knife in his hand cutting her throat, the blood running in a plate for that purpose; and then the scene disappeared: upon which she made all the haste she could to his house, and, finding the door shut, forced it open, when lo! she found the thief in the fang, challenged her mark on the sheep, and then went off; but the thief following her, she became afraid it was with intention to murder her; which instead of attempting, he gave her three or four ells of new linen, which he said was price enough for her sheep, and then strongly recommended to her to keep the whole a secret. From this confession I took occasion to exhort her, by firm faith and earnest prayer, to endeavour to get a sight of her Saviour and Redeemer.

Another story relates to an incident involving one Angus Campbell of Harris:

Angus Campbell, late tacksman of Eansay in Harris, a person of remarkable candour and probity, related, that in a fair sun-shining day, he saw a little fleet, consisting of nine vessels, with an easy leading gale, coming, under sail, to a place called Corminish, opposite to his house, where they dropt their anchors, having their long boats after them, and the crew of each walking the decks; and that his children and several of his domestics took particular notice of a large sloop among them: as the place where they moored in was not a safe harbour, nor that sound a frequented passage to the western ocean, he despatched an express to his servants, who were at a good distance about their labouring, with a view to send a boat to those ships, either to bring them to a safe harbour, or to pilot them out to sea, as they choosed; and, after his servants came up, all of them saw the vessels, as formerly described; but while they were deliberating what to do, the scene disappeared gradually. In two years thereafter, the same number of ships, the remarkable sloop being among them, came and dropt anchor at Corminish, which was attended with all the circumstances above related, according as Eansay told the whole to Mr. Kenneth Macaulay, present Minister of the Harries, from whom I had this relation; and who says there are several still living witnesses of the above representation and its accomplishment.

One of the phenomena associated with the immanent death of another, perceived by the Seer, was to see the person in question shrink to the size of a child, before regaining their normal height. One instance of this was witnessed by John MacLeod, Tacksman of Feorlig. He informed Theophilus that,

> As he and a servant were employed about their labouring, they saw the deceased Mr. John Macleod, late minister of Diurinish, passing by; and having followed him a piece on his way, after they returned to their work, he inquired of his servant, if he observed any remarkable circumstance about the minister? who answered he did, and that he seemed to him, to dwindle away to the bigness of a boy of six or seven years old, and then recover his former size: which my informer having like wise observed, moved him to put the question to his servant. The minister some short time there after sickened, of which he died. And I am told, that this kind of the Second Sight, is commonly the sure forerunner of approaching death.

Another incident related to Theophilus Insulanus was regarding the premonition of a premature death involving the Seer Euphemia Beaton:

> Euphemia Beaton, an honest, sensible, married woman, relates, that, when a girl, and living with her sister the mistress of Feorlig, she rose early in a morning, to make corn ready for grinding; and having brought with her a woman servant, famous for the Second Sight, as they came to the corn-yard, (which is close to the highway,) the servant desired her to keep to a side, as there was a small gathering, with a corps on a bier passing by; she replied that she apprehended no danger, as she had no faith in such predictions; the Seer said, what she had told would soon come to pass; and that her mother and several others she named, would follow the bier, with distinguishing marks of the tartan plaid that lay over the corps. In a few days thereafter, a young man of the neighbourhood was drowned accidentally; the

day before the interment, his body was carried close to the corn-yard, followed by the persons foretold, and attended with all the circumstances above related.

Yet another such incident involved a Major Donald MacLeod:

> Major Donald MacLeod: who had been an officer in the Dutch service, having visited Roderick MacLeod of Hammer, who went along with him to visit William MacLeod of Watersteine, where having passed most of the day, as they were on their way to return, towards the evening, an old woman that lived in a cottage close to the road they passed by, had a view of them; and having met Watersteine as he came back from giving the convoy, inquired who was he that passed by with him and his brother? He told her it was a Dutch officer; upon which she said, they would never see him again, as she saw him shrouded up in his winding sheet, to the crown of his head; which she said was a sure sign of his approaching end. The Major soon thereafter went south, and waiting for a ship at Leith, to transport himself and recruits to Holland, was seized with a fever, of which he died. I had this relation from Watersteine himself, who was a person of unquestionable veracity, and remarkably pious.

Another recorded incident concerned the island of St. Kilda. St. Kilda is an isolated Hebridean archipelago situated 40 miles west-northwest of North Uist in the North Atlantic Ocean. St. Kilda was closely linked to the Isle of Skye through its historical links with Clan MacLeod of Dunvagan.

> Florence MacLeod, spouse to the present minister of St. Kilda, informed me lately, that her mother Elizabeth Macleod, a gentlewoman distinguished from severals for piety and good morals, having come out of her house at Pabbay in the Harris, with a clear moon shining night, and having sat down to enjoy the pleasure of a calm serene air, and the beautiful prospect of a glittering starry firmament, both of them observed a domestic

girl, who had been a native of St. Kilda, (they had left in the house,) issuing from it, covered over with a shroud of a darkish colour, and stalking across the distance betwixt them and the house, as if she intended to frighten them, and after continuing in this manner, for some time, disappeared. Upon their return to the house, the said Elizabeth challenged the girl for her frolic, who affirmed, with many asseverations, she had not left the house all the time her mistress and daughter were absent; to which the other servants gave testimony. In some short time thereafter, the same girl died of a fever, and as there was no linen in the place but what was unbleached, it was made use of for her sowe, which answered the representation exhibited to her mistress and the declarant, as above.

Another correspondent, this time the widow of a St Kildan minister reported that,

> The natives of that island have a particular kind of the Second Sight, which is always a forerunner of their approaching end. Some months before they sicken, they are haunted with an apparition resembling themselves in all respects, as to their person, features or clothing: this image (seemingly animated) walks with them in the fields, in broad day light ; and if they are employed in delving, harrowing, seed-sowing, or any other occupation, they are at the same time mimicked by this ghostly visitant.

Theophilus Insulanus goes on:

> My informer added further, that having visited a sick person of the inhabitants, she had the curiosity to inquire of him, if at any time he had seen any resemblance of himself, as above described? he answered in the affirmative, and told her, that to make further trial, as he was going out of his house on a morning, he put on straw-rope garters, instead of those he formerly used, and having gone to the fields, his other self appeared in

such garters. The conclusion was, the sick man died of that ailment; and she no longer questioned the truth of those remarkable presages.

The township of Unish at the tip of the Waternish peninsula is today totally devoid of habitation. However, it was once home to a thriving community. On one occasion 12-year-old Christian MacDonald was visiting her aunt in Uinish:

> As she (the girl) was coming out of the house, in the dusk of the evening, she saw at the door a gathering of people about a coffin, which so startled her, that she returned to the house, clapping her hands with great cries, and told the company within what she had seen. About a quarter of a year thereafter, her aunt sickened, of which she died, and then the declarant had the opportunity really to see the scene which before had put her into so much fright and confusion.

Another incident which took place in Unish involved one Murdoch MacLeod, 'who, most part of his time, was a tenant in Claiggen, an honest sincere Christian.'

> He related that when Alexander MacLeod of Losgander lived at Uinnish, (he himself being then a married man, having wife and children) being at Uinnish, and on the shore, when Losgander was sending a boat and crew, to ferry cows from the small isles of Uinnish, one Murdoch MacFarlane, obtained leave from his master not to go as one of the crew and when he had left the boat, and came to the place where the declarant stood, he said, he repented not to have gone with the rest; the relater said to him he might go yet, at which he ran as fast as he could, and, as the boat was just going from the rock, he gave a spring to get into her; got his breast on the gunwale of the boat, but his feet sunk into the sea a little above the ancles; and as he was heaving up his feet to get them into the boat, the declarant saw his two soles as red as blood, and said to the bye-standers, that some accident would happen before their return

by what he had seen, which he told publicly. John MacLeod, one of the crew, in their way home from the isles said day, was wounded by one of the cows' horns in the boat: the seer, when they came on shore, saw this man now covered over with real blood. He fevered and died of said wound in a very short time. And this was the second and last time that he saw the Second Sight which had its completion the same day it appeared to his imagination.

The following is a story related to Theophilus Insulanus by one 'Mrs. Anderson from Kilmuir':

In spring 1751, as she lay awake in her bed in Kilmuir, (the rest of the family being all asleep), she heard a great noise behind the partition of deals that was close to her bed-head ; she imagined that part of the wall of the house had fallen, called to her son to get up, and to go out to see if the wall was fallen; which he declining, she, in a few minutes, went out, viewed the wall which stood firm, and so disappointed her expectation. Same night Florence Beaton, her servant-maid, dreamed, that Donald MacCaskill, present beadle, their door-neighbour, carried a large white mutton into his own house, and hung it up. About sun rise that morning, John MacLeod of Drynoch, and his servant, coming from Dunvegan, went by the end of the house, and about the sixth part of an English mile in the sight of the houses, the servant shot himself accidentally with his master's fusee; his corpse was carried by Donald MacCaskill and others, into his own house: the gun and wallet he carried, were laid at the partition in Mrs. Anderson's, and the dale where she heard most of the noise, was taken down, and the corpse laid thereon ; thus both the noise and dream, had their completion in three or four hours.

The book *A Treatise On The Second Sight, Dreams and Apparitions* has many more attested incidents which took place on the Isle of Skye and other places. Another one must suffice for the present chapter. It relates to a dream revelation which was to reward its recipient financially.

> Kenneth Morison, of good repute with his cotemporaries, then living at Glendale, had a revelation in a dream, as follows: A person informed him in sleep, that if he should repair to the kirk of Kilchoan, and look out at the east window, he might see at the distance of two pair of butts, in a direct line eastward, a stone larger than any near it in that direction; upon re moving of which, he would find silver, which had been hid under it : and accordingly he lost no time, but went the next day to take his observation as he was directed ; and, having found out the stone, was not disappointed, as it overlay a heap of silver under it of different size, coinage and value; a part of which was not then of the common currency. I had formerly this story given me for certain; but the above narration was lately confirmed to me by Alexander Morison, an elder in the parish of Diurinish, and grandchild to the said Kenneth, who had it delivered to him from Doctor Donald Morison, his own father, in substance the same with what is already mentioned.

ENDNOTES

1. Ferguson appears to have entered the Scots brigade in the pay of Holland, probably as a gentleman volunteer, some time during the reign of Charles II. His first commission, that of quartermaster in Colonel Macdonald's battalion of the brigade, was dated 12 June 1677. He became ensign in the battalion in September 1678, and lieutenant in February 1682. His battalion was one of those brought over to England in 1685 at the time of Monmouth's rebellion. He became captain in 1687, and in 1688 landed with William of Orange at Torbay. His regiment, then known as Balfour's and afterwards as Lauder's, was one of those first landed, and soon after despatched from London to Leith under Mackay. The fight at Killiecrankie, where he is said to have been taken prisoner, left him a regimental major; and in March 1690 he was despatched by General Mackay, who described him as 'a resolute, well-affected officer,' in whose discretion and diligence he had full reliance, at the head of six hundred men, to reduce the western isles, a service he accomplished satisfactorily with the aid of the Glasgow authorities and the co-operation of Captain Pottinger of the Dartmouth frigate. (James Ferguson, *Two Scottish Soldiers* (Aberdeen, 1888) pp. 15-16.

2. Possibly Father Ryan, one of the seven Catholic priests who had established themselves in the Highlands prior to the 1688–9 revolution. See - Leith, *Memoirs of the Scottish Catholics*, ii, 169. Quoted in - Michael Hunter, *The Occult Laboratory, Magic, Science and Second Sight in Late Seventeenth-Century Scotland*, (Boydell & Brewer, Boydell Press) 2001, p.195.

3. The Battle of Killiecrankie took place on 27 July 1689 during the 1689 Scottish Jacobite rising. An outnumbered Jacobite force under John Graham, Viscount Dundee and Sir Ewen Cameron of Lochiel defeated a government army commanded by General Hugh Mackay. James VII went into exile in December 1688 after being deposed by the Glorious Revolution in Scotland.

CHAPTER 3

Prince & Prophets

*The child saw the house on fire, soon set both kiln and house in a flame,
which they soon extinguished: and at the same time verified the child's
vision, within two hours after she saw it.*

Theophilus Insulanus (c1763)

Many of the incidents we are looking at here, as we
suggested earlier, took place at a time of great unrest
and uncertainty in the Hebrides in general. At the time of
the first of the next two stories, the Jacobite uprising had
just come to an end. In the second, the premonition, some
two years before the event, was fulfilled again, just after the
battle of Culloden in 1746, when government troops were
scouring the Hebrides in search of 'The Young Pretender',
Prince Charles Edward Stuart. Theophilus Insulanus records:

> Mr. Andrson, assured me, that upon the sixteenth
> day of April, 1746, (being the day on which his Royal
> Highness the Duke of Cumberland obtained a glorious

victory over the rebels at Culloden,) as he lay in bed with his spouse, towards the dawning of the day, he heard very audibly, a voice at his bed-head, inquiring, if he was awake? who answered, he was, but then took no further notice of it. A little time thereafter, the voice repeated, with greater vehemence, if he was awake? And he answering, as formerly, he was: there was some stop, when the voice repeated louder, asking the same question, and he making the same answer; but added, what the voice had to say; upon which it replied, The Prince is defeated, defeated, defeated! And in less than forty-eight hours thereafter, an express carried the welcome tidings of the fact into the country.

So much then for the sometimes-promoted romantic view in our own day that sees almost universal support for the Jacobite cause among the people of the Highlands and Hebrides. The true picture is much more complex.

In the year 1744, Lauchlane Macculloch, then servant to Alexander Macdonald of Gearry Dhonil, in Bein-Bicula, (Benbecula) coming out of his master's house under night, before he had gone many paces, there appeared to him, at no great distance, a promiscuous heap of red-coats, and Highlandmen, on the path that led to the house, which sight so frighted him, that in the hurry he was in to get back to the house, he struck his shin against a stone to the effusion of his blood; and immediately, as soon as he entered, told what he had seen to his fellow servants. In 1746, Captain Ferguson, who commanded the Furnace sloop of war, at the head of a corps of the troops, and Argyle militia, came to Gearry-Dhonil's house, which gave an opportunity to all that were in the family to see them really, as Macculloch hed seen them about two years before, by the Second Sight. I had this relation from Alexander Macdonald, son to the above Gearry Dhonil, a good sensible, modest young man, who acknowledged to me, that Macculloch owned to have seen the Sight as it came to pass.

Interestingly we know that Bonnie Prince Charlie had arrived at night in Benbecula on 20th April 1746 from where he subsequently walked to Borradale, South Uist. Between 22-25th April he stayed in the neighbourhood of Borradale while one Donald MacLeod procured a boat and a crew. He thereafter travelled to 'Lewis, Harris, Uist and Western Mainland.' He returned to Loch Boisdale, South Uist on or about the 20th of June, hiding thereafter in the mountains. On 21st June the Prince arrived at a hut, near Ormaclett, at midnight, where his group met Flora MacDonald and asked her assistance to convey the Prince to Skye, which she agreed to do. On 28th June, in the evening, the Prince dressed in female clothing as 'Betty Burke', Flora's servant, was joined by Flora MacDonald, and sailed for Skye. The party consisted of the Prince, Flora MacDonald, Neil MacEachain, and four boatmen. On 29th June the party arrived off the point of Waternish in Skye but found the place occupied by troops, who fired on them. They rowed off and rested in concealment in a creek; then rowed on to Kilbride in Trotternish where they landed near 'Mougstot' (Monkstadt) House. Flora went directly to Lady Margaret MacDonald at Monkstat, who sent her factor, MacDonald of Kingsburgh (Flora's future father-in-law), to the Prince with refreshments. The Prince walked with him to Kingsburgh House, where he spent the night. Kingsburgh house was of course also the home of Allan MacDonald, (son of Alexander MacDonald) mentioned earlier in relation to his correspondence with William MacLeod, and the future husband of Flora MacDonald.[1]

However, from this point on, things would go horribly wrong for Flora. Foolishly, in hindsight, the boat and crew that had recently taken them to Skye returned immediately to Uist where they were at once apprehended, interrogated and admitted to all they knew. James Ferguson immediately set sail for Skye in search of the Prince but lost trace of him at Portree.

Meanwhile, Flora had returned to her mother's home in Sleat. Some 10 days thereafter, however, she was lured into a trap by being asked to visit a nearby house. This trap was apparently set by one John MacLeod of Talisker, captain of an 'Independent Company'[2] – and the house to which she was lured belonged to one 'Donald MacDonald of Castleton'. On route to the house she was 'seized by an officer and party of soldiers, and hurried on board Captain Ferguson's cutter, the Furnace'.[3] Some 20 days later and still on board she was allowed, under escort, to visit her friends at Armadale and collect some clothing. She was thereafter held as a prisoner for a short time at Dunstaffnage Castle Dunbeg, near Oban. She is described in prison records as 'A very pretty rebel, 24 years of age'.[4] On the 28th of December 1846 she was transferred to the ship *Royal Sovereign* – and taken to custody in London. She was eventually released at the passing of the Act of Indemnity in July 1747.

About two weeks after the Prince had been sheltered at Kingsburgh House, Ferguson arrived with his troops and arrested Alexander MacDonald. On arrival at Fort Augustus MacDonald was 'thrown into a dungeon and, loaded with chains.'[5] He was subsequently removed to Edinburgh Castle and held in solitary confinement, only being released from custody on the 4th of July 1747 under the same act as that which preceded the release of his future daughter-in-law – Flora MacDonald.

Alexander MacDonald of Kingsburgh (1689–1772), Allan's father, mentioned above,[6] is also known to have prophetic dreams. His son Allan recorded the following regarding him in the letter referred to earlier.

> Alexander MacDonald of Kingsborough, (when living in the possession of Aird, in the remote end of Trotternish,) dreamed that he saw an old reverend man come to him, desiring him to get out of bed, and get his servants together, and make haste to save his corns, as his own whole cattle, and his tenants' cattle also, had got out of the fold, and were in the middle of a large field behind the house; he awaked and told his

wife, with whom he consulted whether he would rise or not; and she telling him it was but a dream, and not worth noticing, advising him to lie still, which he obeyed; but no sooner fell asleep, than the former old man appeared to him, and seemed angry, by telling Mr. MacDonald, (then of Aird) he the old man was very idle, in acquainting him of the loss he would or had by this time sustained by his cattle, and seemed not to heed what he said, and so went off. Mr. MacDonald awaking the second time, told this to his wife, and would be at rising in any event, but she would not allow him, and ridiculed him for noticing the folly of a confused dream; so that, after attempting to get up, he was, at his wife's persuasion, prevailed upon to lie down again; and falling asleep, it being now near break of day, the old gentleman appeared to him the third time, with a frowning countenance, and told him he might now lie still, for that the cattle were now surfeited of his corn, were lying in it; and that it was for his welfare that he came to acquaint him so often, as he was his granduncle by the father; and so went off. He awakening in about an hour thereafter, arose and went out, and actually found his own and his tenants' cattle lying in his corn, after being tired of eating thereof; which corn, when comprised, the loss amounted to eight bolls of meal.

Another incident connected with the Jacobite rising relates to a visit to Moy, near Inverness, by Bonnie Prince Charlie. Lady Anne Mackintosh of Moy Hall, who had helped 'the Young Pretender' raise men for the Jacobite cause, entertained him and his men. It was at this time that the Prince narrowly avoided capture at the hands of his enemies. To prevent troops from Inverness making a surprise descent on the estate during the night, Lady Anne Farquharson-Mackintosh sent Donald Fraser the blacksmith and four other retainers to watch the road from Inverness. Sure enough, during the night several hundred Hanoverian troops were detected marching down the road. The Mackintosh defenders started beating their swords on rocks, jumping from place to place and shouting the war cries of different clans in the Chattan confederation. Thinking that they had been ambushed, the Government troops retreated leaving Inverness open for the Prince to capture the next day, an event known as the 'Rout of Moy'.

Connected to this incident, as we have indicated, and one other, is yet another premonition recorded in a letter to Theophilus Insulanus:

> Patrick MacCaskill, an honest country farmer, of good report with all his neighbours, who deserves credit as much as any churchman of the most unblemished morals, and is mentioned in the body of this treatise, declared to me, that, in the evening before the Earl of Loudon attempted to surprise the young Pretender, at the castle of Moy, Donald Maccrummen, piper to the independent company, (commanded by the young Laird of Macleod,) talked with him on the street of Inverness, where they were under arms, to march, they did not know whither, as their expedition was kept a secret: and that, after the said Donald, a goodly person, six feet high, parted with him about pistol-shot, he saw him all at once contracted to the bigness of a boy of five or six years old, and immediately, with the next look, resume his former size. The same night Maccrummen was accidently shot dead on their long march, which concluded the operation of that night's enterprize. The same person informed me, that, being a soldier in the corps commanded by the old laird of MacLeod, at the unfortunate skirmish of Inverury, one Normand MacLeod, a serjeant of their corps, fell in discourse with him, after returning from viewing some posts supposed to be occupied by the enemy; and that, notwithstanding the serjeant was of a ruddy plump complexion, he appeared to him then of a ghastly aspect, his eyes sunk in their sockets, and all his visage pale as death; and, with a second look, saw him recover his bloom, which was pure red and white. In less than an hour thereafter, they were alarmed with the enemy's fire, and having come to an action, which lasted several hours, the serjeant for some time maintained an unequal fight against two or

three, but, in the end, being overpowered, fell among the slain: which verified the Second Sight and presage, seen by him before the engagement.

Moving on for a moment to the mainland, opposite Skye – to the village of Glenelg, Theophilus Insulanus relates a number of incidents involving a Seer known as Sergeant.

There lives at Glenelg a person commonly known by the name of Sergeant, a most remarkable Seer, of whom I had many stories, from very good authors, of his prophetic talent: I will only mention one, which may serve as a sample of all the rest, and was delivered to me by Ensign MacLeod, who, as he was travelling home under night, accompanied by the Sergeant, this Seer, on the sudden, desired him to keep to a side, as there was a throng gathering of people coming on the direct path of the road, carrying a corpse on a litter. The ensign having told him he had no faith in such discoveries, the Seer replied, the vision in a short time would be fulfilled, and that the ensign himself would be one of the company; and then named severals from the neighbouring countries, distinguishing them by their names, arms, and clothing, who were to assist at the interment; and pointed at particular passes, where such and such men were to relieve those who carried the bier. In some short time thereafter, a gentlewoman that was sister to the ensign, departed this life, at Myle in Glenmore: all the persons foretold, were called and assisted at the interment, without the least variation from the scene, as above described, from the declarant's observation, who took notice of the particular circumstances communicated to him by the Seer. And if of the curious should wish for more instananyces of his predictions, he may apply to the Reverend Mr. Donald MacLeod, minister of Glenelg, who may furnish him with severals, as he has a throng collection of surprising narrations, delivered him by the Serjeant.

Another incident involving a soldier took place in north Skye:

> As a further illustration of this particular, give me leave
> to mention a very remarkable instance, as I had it from
> Lieutenant Armstrong, a gentleman (by all I ever could
> learn) tender of his honour, and who, with a liberal
> education, under the awful influence of religion, and
> the strictest morals, joins the Christian with the soldier.
> He relates, that, in his way to visit MacLeod from
> Portree, as he was crossing the hill Hornievall, above
> Loun-a-Chlerish, he saw a soldier in the regimentals
> of his corps, in that bottom; and thereupon inquired
> of his servant, if he saw him? Who answered, No; tho'
> they walked together, and looked the same way. The
> gentleman added, the vision did not disappear at once,
> but gradually: when he and his servant came down to
> the bottom, they examined narrowly, if there were any
> cattle feeding thereabout, yet could meet with none, till
> they arrived at Dunvegan. From which it is plain, the
> scene was not deceptiovisus, to mistake one object for
> another, ' but (as said is) exhibited to the imagination.
> The next day he had account from Portree, by express,
> of his serjeant's death, the day before, about the time
> he saw him on Loun-a-Chlerish, by a waking dream,
> which I take to be the best definition of the Second
> Sight.

But to return to the Glenelg area, a place closely connected with
the Isle of Skye, due to it being one of the shortest crossing points
between the island and the Mainland, we have yet another story
recounted by Theophilus Insulanus:

> Being informed, that one John MacKay, a poor old
> man, living at Laoran in Glenelg, made no secret
> of having seen an apparition, I had the curiosity to
> call for him, to know the truth of a report that had
> prevailed, of his getting intelligence of future events;
> on that occasion, having obeyed my summons, and
> as I perceived that time had furrowed his visage, the
> first question I asked was about his age; which he said

was about one hundred. I then proceeded to inquire of him, if he had met such a spirit as was commonly reported, and how he was entertained by him. Upon which he frankly acknowledged, that after night-fall, as he was coming home to his house in 1745, he heard a voice calling after him, Where was he going? To which he replied, that he was returning home to his house; and asked the voice, how far, and what route he was to travel? Who answered, he was to seek his mantle that lay near a rivulet hard by. This answer gave my informer a suspicion his new correspondent was more than human: and presently inquired, how it was to happen in these perilous times, to several chiefs of clans, and particularly to the old and young Barisdales, who were much in his esteem, as they were the most considerable persons in his neighbourhood: answer was returned to his several questions, but in such a mysterious enigmatical way as made the meaning very uncertain, and only conjectural. However, the old sage decyphered the words so as to correspond with the conduct and circumstances of those for whom they were intended. I asked, If he had seen the representation of what spoke with him, or if the voice seemed human? He answered in the negative to the first, and that the latter was more shrill than usually proceeds from material organs. Ensign Donald MacLeod, and his brother Normand, persons of candour, who lived then at Laoran, informed me, that, having missed a cow for nine or ten days, which being sought out in vain by his herd, he at length coming accidentally to the said John MacKay's house, and having made mention to him of the cow that was lost or strayed; he told him, that he would find her perished in a certain spot, mangled by dogs at both ends, and directed to the place, with such marks of the situation, rocks and trees that were adjoining, that, without any mistake, he came to it, and found the cow, as described by old John, who had been for five weeks confined to his bed, and his wife absent all the time; so that he had no means to know any thing about the cow, but either from the Second Sight, or some other method of divination. The said Ensign informed me, that, having gone with his wife to visit his father-in-law in the isle of Sky, night coming on, they were obliged to put up with a cave on the side of Lough Urn, to pass the night; and, as they were at supper, his wife took cabbock of cheese in her hand, and, having covered it with three or four apples, wished it in a Seer's hand, who lived with her father; and who, that night, by the Second Sight, saw the gentlewoman offering her a cabbock of cheese, but was at a loss to know what the round things were that covered it, as perhaps she had seen none of the kind in her lifetime, until her master's daughter, upon her arrival, told her the whole.

Moving south for a moment to Islay, the southernmost island of the Inner Hebrides. Islay is sometimes known as 'The Queen of the Hebrides' and is within Argyllshire, just southwest of Jura and around 22 nautical miles north of the Northern Irish coast. Theophilus Insulanus records:

In the year 1723, or 1724, there lived in the island of Isla, Angus MacMillan, an honest conscientious country farmer, in good esteem with all his acquaintances. He, and my informer, happened to meet on a day at Mr. Donald Campbell's house,(Macmillan's landlord); Mr. Campbell upbraided him (in joke) with the name of Seer, &c. He made answer, that, though he was not of that tribe, he ought not to jest for his diversion on such a serious subject ; however, he could tell him of an event which was to happen that same day, in which he was the principal person concerned; and then told him, in presence of the company, he would break his leg before he arrived at Sunderland's, about a mile's distance. Mrs. Campbell hearing this prophecy, desired Mr. Camphell to stay at home for that day; but he laughed at her credulity, caused her to bring him a dram to drink to the Seer, and immediately took his horse (that stood saddled at the door); MacMillan, and my informer, following on foot, found him sprawling on the sand, and his leg broken, by a fall of horse and rider; where upon they laid him on a bier brought from the church, and carried him with the help of others to Sunderland's house, where a doctor being accidentally, set his leg; my informer, (a person of great candour) and MacMillan himself assisting at the operation.

We end this chapter by returning to two more connected stories from Skye as recorded, once again, by Theophilus Insulanus:

Alexander Dingwall, an honest tenant in Waternish, in September, 1761, contracted the bloody-flux, accompanied with a most violent grinding: towards the end of said month he went out a little before day, to look about his corn in the corn-yard; as he was returning to his house he heard very grievous lamentations, which appeared to him to begin at the end of his own house, and continued, as he imagined, all the way to the shore. How soon he came in he told all to his wife and children; his stepdaughter, who came in just before him, said, as that morning had a raw frost, the voice which he heard must be that of a fox, to cause dogs run after to give him heat: no, child, said Alexander, it is my spirit or ghost, and I will never set a foot on green grass more. This was seen verified, his disease increasing so fast and violent upon him, that in eight or ten days he departed this life, and the mourning of his wife, children, and friends, accompanied his corpse from the door to the shore, (about a quarter of a mile,) where it was put in the boat to be interred at Killmuir.

Elizabeth Dingwall, daughter to the above Alexander, a child about five years old, as she was washing her face and hands, beginning of harvest last, cried out to her mother, saying, see, mother, the house is on fire: her mother and all the family looking that way, could see no such thing; she reproved the child for surprising them with lies; but the child still persisted in her affirmation. In less than two hours thereafter, a neighbouring women coming in with some shingles of barley to be dried on the small kiln, that stood under the very place where the child saw the house on fire, soon set both kiln and house in a flame, which they soon extinguished: and at the same time verified the child's vision, within two hours after she saw it.[7]

ENDNOTES

1. Alan and Flora MacDonald are believed to have been married on 6th November 1750 in Armidale Castle, Sleat.

2. Independent Companies were forces raised by Clan Chiefs loyal to the British Crown. For instance, Norman MacLeod, chief of the Clan MacLeod, led 500 men of the MacLeod Independent Highland Companies at the Battle of Inverurie where they were defeated by a numerically superior Jacobite force on 23rd December 1745. It is said that, on occasions, the men enlisted in to these companies did not know whether or not they would be fighting for King George and the British forces or the Jacobites under Prince Charles Edward Stuart. The John MacLeod referred to in relation to the capture of Flora MacDonald was the son of Norman MacLeod of Dunvegan, chief of Clan MacLeod.

3. Alexander Cameron, *The History and Traditions of the Isle of Skye,* (E. Forsyth, Bank Street, Inverness, 1871) pp.118 – 119. Cameron would appear to be mistaken in identifying Ferguson as 'Captain'. He was in fact a Colonel at this point in his career and not Captain of the vessel, as Cameron seems to imply.

4. William Mackenzie, *Old Skye Tales,* (First edition 1930 – reprinted by MacLean Press, Skye 1995) p. 68.

5. Alexander Cameron, *The History and Traditions of the Isle of Skye,* (E. Forsyth, Bank Street, Inverness.) 1871 p.138.

6. Alexander MacDonald was 6th of Kingsburgh. Alexander was appointed, in 1718, Chamberlain for Sir Donald MacDonald's Totternish lands. He acquired a tack for Knockcowe and Kilvaxter in 1722, and later, in 1734 he gave up these holdings in favour of Kingsburgh. Though he was the first of his family to hold the Kingsburgh estate the family are none the less known by that designation.

7. This story reflects one known to the author, as is the person involved. A few years ago in north Skye a young girl had a dream in which her father's works truck, which he always parked very close to the wall of the family home overnight, went on fire and burned down the house. She told her parents who dismissed it as a child's dream. However, the next evening when

her father parked his vehicle as normal - she begged him to move it. In order to put her mind at rest he eventually moved the vehicle some distance away from the house. Overnight it did catch fire - and had it been parked in its normal location it would, at the very least, have caused substantial damage to the house and perhaps worse.

CHAPTER 4

Martin Martin

All the neighbours condemned Archibald as a foolish prophet: upon which, he passionately affirmed, that if ever that sick man dies in the house where he now lies, I shall from henceforth renounce my part of heaven.

Martin Martin (c1700)

Another rich source of evidence in relation to our subject, as we mentioned earlier, is to be found in the book, published in 1703, by Martin Martin - *A Description of the Western Islands of Scotland.*

Martin was a native Gaelic speaker from Skye who, in the 1690s, became convinced of the need for a first-hand account of the society, culture and natural history of the Western Isles. Of the premonition of an impending death in the Hebrides he records:

> There is a way of foretelling death by a cry that they call
> Taisk, which some call a Wraith in the lowland. They

hear a loud cry without doors, exactly resembling the voice of some particular person, whose death is foretold by it. The last instance given me of this kind was in the village Rigg, in the isle of Sky. Five women were sitting together in the same room, and all of them heard a loud cry passing by the window; they thought it plainly to be the voice of a maid who was one of the number: she blushed at the time, though not sensible of her so doing, contracted a fever next day, and died that week.

As well as people, Martin was convinced that animals also could perceive the presence of the spiritual. He records:

A horse fastened by the common road on the side of Loch-Skeriness in Sky, did break his rope at noon-day, and ran up and down without the least visible cause. But two of the neighbourhood that happened to be at a little distance, and in view of the horse, did at the same time see a considerable number of men about a corps, directing their course to the church of Snisort; and this was accomplished within a few days after, by the death of a gentlewoman who lived thirteen miles from that church, and came from another parish, from whence very few come to Snisort to be buried.

Recording an incident which had taken place in Flodigarry he reported:

Four men of the village Flodgery in Sky, being at supper, one of them did suddenly let fall his knife on the table, and looked with an angry countenance: the company observing it, inquired his: reason but he returned them no answer until they had supped, and then he told them that when he let fall his knife, he saw a corps with the shroud about it laid on the table, which surprised him, and that a little time would accomplish the vision. It fell out accordingly, for in a few days after, one of the family died, and happened to be laid on that very table. This was told me by the master of the family.

At times incidents are recorded of a vision or dream being experienced by a person only once in their lives, Such is the case in the following incident recorded by Martin:

> Daniel Stuart an inhabitant of Hole in the north parish of St. Maries in the isle of Sky, saw at noon-day five men on horseback riding north-ward; he ran to meet them, and when he came to the road, he could see none of them, which was very surprising to him, and he told it his neighbours: the next day he saw the same number of men and horse coming along the road, but was not so ready to meet them as before, until he heard them speak, and then he found them to be those that he had seen the day before in a vision; this was the only vision of the kind he had ever seen in his life. The company he saw was Sir Donald MacDonald and his retinue, who at the time of the vision was at Armidil, near forty miles south from the place where the man lived.

Martin also related an incident involving a Seer, Daniel Dow from 'Bernskittag' in the north of the island who was,

> Frequently troubled at the sight of a man threatening to give him a blow: he knew no man resembling this vision; but the stature, complexion, and babit, were so impressed on his mind, that he said he could distinguish him from any other, if he should happen to see him. About a year after the vision appeared first to him, his master sent him to Kyle-raes, above thirty miles further south-east, where he was no sooner arrived, than he distinguished the man who had so often appeared to him at home; and within a few hours after, they happened to quarrel, and came to blows, so as one of them (I forgot which) was wounded in the head. This was told me by the Seer's master, and others who live in the place. The man himself has his residence there, and is one of the precisest Seers in the isles.

Martin goes on to record of Dow:

Daniel Dow above-named, foretold the death of a young woman in Minginis, within less than twenty-four hours before the time; and accordingly she died suddenly in the fields, though at the time of the prediction she was in perfect health; but the shroud appearing close about her head, was the ground of his confidence, that her death was at hand. The same Daniel Dow foretold the death of a child in his master's arms, by seeing a spark of fire fall on his left arm; and this was likewise accomplished soon after the prediction.

Another incident recorded by Martin is somewhat unusual:

Some of the inhabitants of Harries (Harris) sailing round the isle of Sky, with a design to go to the opposite main land, were strangely surprised with an apparition of two men hanging down by the ropes that secured the mast, but could not conjecture what it meant. They pursued the voyage, but the wind turned contrary, and so forced them into Broadford in the isle of Sky, where they found Sir Donald MacDonald keeping a Sheriff's Court, and two criminals receiving sentence of death there: the ropes and mast of that very boat were made use of to hang those criminals. This was told me by several, who had this instance from the boat's crew.

Rank, position or standing appears to have been no defence against the penetrating vision of the Seer, as is witnessed in the following incident recorded by Martin:

My Lord Viscount Tarbat, one of her majesty's secretaries of state in Scotland, travelling in the shire of Ross, in the north of Scotland, came into a house, and sat down in an armed chair: one of his retinue who had the faculty of seeing the Second Sight, spoke to some of my Lord's company, desiring them to persuade him to leave the house; for, said he, there is a great misfortune will attend somebody in it, and that within a few hours. This was told my lord, but he did not regard it: the Seer did soon after renew his intreaty, with much eagerness, begging that my lord might remove out of that unhappy chair, but had no other answer than to be exposed for a fool. Some hours after my lord removed, and pursued his journey; but was not gone many hours when a trooper riding upon the ice, near the house whence my lord re- moved, fell and broke his thigh, and being after wards brought in that house, was laid in the armed chair, where his wound was dressed, which accomplished the vision. I heard this instance from several hands, and had it since confirmed by my lord himself.

In his book *The Secret Commonwealth,* Robert Kirk (1644-1692), a minister, Gaelic scholar and Folklorist, tells a very interesting story related to him by Sir Norman Macleod of Harris:

Among the accounts given Me by Sir Normand McCleud, there was one worthy of special notice, which was thus. There was a Gentlman in the Isle of Harris, who was always seen by the Seers, with ane arrow in his Thigh. Such in the Isle who thought those prognostications infallible did not doubt but he would be shot in the thigh befor he died. Sir Normand told me that he heard it the subject of their discourse for many years. When that Gentlman was present. At last he died without anie such accident, Sir Normand was at his Burial at Saint Clements Church in the Harris. At the same time the Corps of another Gentlman was brought to be buried in the same verie Church. The friends on aither side came to debate who should first enter the Church and in a trice from words they came to Blous. One of the number (who was arm'd with Bow and Arrows) Let one fly among them. (Now every Familie in that Isle have their burial place in the Church in stonechests, and the Bodies are caryed in open Biers to the Burial-place.) Sir Normand having appeased the Tumult one of the arrows was found shot in the dead mans thigh. To this Sir Normand himselfe was a witness.

But to return again to a number of stories involving north Skye, recorded by Martin Martin:

A man in the parish of St. Maries, in the barony of Troterness in Sky, called Lachlin, lay sick for the space of some months, decaying daily, insomuch that all his relations and acquaintance despaired of his recovery. One of the parishioners, called Archibald MacDonald, being reputed famous for his skill in foretelling things to come, by the Second Sight, asserted positively that the sick man would never die in the house where he then lay. This being thought very improbable, all the neighbours condemned Archibald as a foolish prophet: upon which, he passionately affirmed, that if ever that sick man dies in the house where he now lies, I shall from henceforth renounce my part of heaven; adding withal, the sick man was to be carried alive out of the house in which he then lay, but that he would never return to it alive; and then he named the persons that should carry out the sick man alive. The man having lived some weeks longer than his friends imagined, and proving uneasy and troublesome to all the family; they considered that Archibald had reason for his peremptory assertion, and therefore they resolved to carry him to a house joining to that in which he then lay but the poor man would by no means give his consent to be moved from a place where he believed he should never die; so much did he rely on the words of Archibald, of whose skill he had seen many demonstrations. But at last his friends being fatigued day and night with the sick man's uneasiness, they carried him against his inclination to another little house, which was only separated by an entry from that in which he lay, and their feet were scarce within the threshold, when the sick man gave up the ghost; and it was remarkable that the two neighbours, which Archibald named would carry him out, were actually the persons that did so. At the time of the prediction, Archibald saw him carried out as above, and when he was within the door of the other house, he saw him all white, and the shroud being about him, occasioned his confidence as above mentioned. This is matter of fact, which Mr. Daniel Nicholson, minister of the parish, and a considerable number of the parishioners, are able to vouch for, and ready to attest, if occasion requires.

The same Archibald MacDonald happened to be in the village Knockow one night, and before supper told the family, that he had just then seen the strangest thing he ever saw in his life; to wit, a man with an ugly long cap, always shaking his head but that the strangest of all, was a little kind of a harp which he had, with four strings only; and that it had two harts-horns fixed in the front of it. All that heard this odd vision, fell a laughing at Archibald, telling him that he was dreaming, or had not his wits about him; since he pretended to see a thing that had no being, and was not so much as heard of in any part of the world. All this could not alter Archibald's opinion, who told them that they must excuse him, if he laughed at them after the accomplishment of the vision. Archibald returned to his own house, and within three or four days after, a man with the cap, harp, &c. came to the house, and the harp, strings, horns, and cap, answered the description of them at first view: he shook his head when he played, for he had two bells fixed to his cap. This harper was a poor man, and made himself a buffoon for his bread, and was never before seen in those parts; for at the time of the prediction, he was in the isle of Barra, which is above twenty leagues distant from that part of Sky. This story is vouched by Mr. Daniel Martin, and all his family, and such as were then present, and live in the village where this happened.

Mr. Daniel Nicholson, minister of St. Maries in Sky, the parish in which Archibald MacDonald lived, told me, that one Sunday after sermon, at the chapel Uge, he took occasion to inquire of Archibald, if he still retained that unhappy faculty of seeing the Second Sight, and he wished him to lay it aside, if possible; for, said he, it is no true character of a good man. Archibald was highly displeased, and answered, that he hoped he was no more unhappy than his neighbours, for seeing what they could not perceive; adding, I had, says he, as serious thoughts as my neighbours, in time of hearing a sermon to-day, and even then I saw a corps laid on the ground close to the pulpit, and I assure you it will be accomplished shortly, for it was in the daytime.

Mr. Nicholson and several parishioners then present, endeavoured to dissuade Archibald from this discourse; but he still asserted that it would quickly come to pass, and that all his other predictions of this kind had ever been accomplished. There was none in the parish then sick, and few are buried at that little chapel, nay sometimes not one in a year is buried there; yet when Mr. Nicholson returned to preach in the said chapel, two or three weeks after, he found one buried in the very spot named by Archibald. This story is vouched by Mr. Nicholson, and several of the parishioners still living.

Mr. Daniel Nicholson above-mentioned, being a widower at the age of forty-four, this Archibald saw in a vision a young gentlewoman, in a good dress, frequently standing at Mr. Nicholson's right hand, and this he often told the parishioners positively; and gave an account of her complexion, stature, habit, and that she would in time be Mr. Nicholson's wife: this being told the minister by several of them, he desired them to have no regard to what that foolish dreamer had said; for, said he, it is twenty to one if ever I marry again. Archibald happened to see Mr. Nicholson soon after this slighting expression, however he persisted still in his opinion, and said confidently that Mr. Nicholson would certainly marry, and that the woman would in all points make up the character he gave of her, for he saw her as often as he saw Mr. Nicholson. This story was told me above a year before the accomplishment of it; and Mr. Nicholson, some two or three years after Archibald's prediction, went to a synod in Bute, where he had the first opportunity of seeing one Mrs. Morison, and from that moment fancied her, and afterwards married her. She was no sooner seen in the isle of Sky, than the natives, who had never seen her before, were satisfied that she did completely answer the character given of her, &c. by Archibald.

Finally, Martin also tells us about a very unusual incident which took place on the Isle of Bernera.

Sir Normand MacLeod, who has his residence in the isle of Bernera, which lies between the isle of North-Uist and Harries, went to the isle of Sky about business, without appointing any time for his return: his servants in his absence, being altogether in the large hall at night, one of them who had been accustomed to see the Second Sight, told the rest they must remove, for they would have abundance of other company in the hall that night. One of his fellow-servants answered, that there was very little appearance of that, and if he had seen any vision of company, it was not like to be accomplished this night: but the Seer insisted upon it, that it was. They continued to argue the improbability of it, because of the darkness of the night, and the danger of coming through the rocks that lie round the isle but within an hour after, one of Sir Normand's men came to the house, bidding them provide lights, &c. for his master had newly landed and thus the prediction was immediately accomplished.

CHAPTER 5

Sceptics & Kings

God was pleased to make him an example of, to show that the Infinite God is not to be limited in his all-wise operations, by the erring confined conceptions of human understanding.

Theophilus Insulanus (c1763)

One sceptic that Theophilus Insulanus, author of *The Second Sight*, could not win over to his point of view was fellow minister, Donald MacLeod. However, MacLeod was himself to become the subject of a premonition concerning his own demise. Theophilus records:

> Having frequently had occasion to converse with the late Reverend Mr. Donald MacLeod, minister of the gospel, anent the Second Sight, I could not, with all my philosophy, the force of my arguments, or from any instances which give credit to that kind of prediction, convince him there was any truth in them but he always insisted those seeming intimations were the pure offspring of ignorance or enthusiastic credulity;

and always advanced, we were to trust to a more sure word of prophecy, as if he had believed that revelation by dreams and visions was entirely ceased; and yet this person, who in all other respects was, more than most of men, (without being divinely inspired) remarkable for extensive benevolence and sanctity of manners; God was pleased to make him an example of, to show that the Infinite God is not to be limited in his all-wise operations, by the erring confined conceptions of human understanding : for, about a fortnight before he departed this life, one Archibald MacLean, his servant, (who had never before seen the Second Sight,) as he was going in, under night, to a room in the closet, before he entered, saw, through a chink in the leaf, that chamber illuminated with an extraordinary blaze of light, and, having entered, saw a corpse stretched on a dale that stood in the room, dressed up in his winding-sheet; which having told next day among his fellow-servants, the minister at length was in formed of it, who, having called for the Seer, and examined him on what he had seen, he owned and affirmed the scene for truth; upon which the minister said he did not believe it, though he never knew him before to have told a lie. The mistress of the house being present, in order to expose the vanity of the Second Sight, resolved to employ that dale in some immediate use, and ordered it to be laid aside; but before that was done the minister fevered, of which he died in six days, and that very dale was laid under his corpse after it was washen. Of all which I was informed by the Seer himself, by the relict (widow), and the defunct's brother.

Another such story involving a minister was reported by one Roderick MacLeod 'a plain good-natured young man.' He informed Theophilus Insulanus:

That when he served the deceased reverend Mr. John Macleod, sometime minister of Diurinish, in the station of an overseer, as he was going into the principal house in the dusk of the evening, met the said Mr. John coming out, who came so close to him as to touch the declarant's clothes, as he imagined; but having entered the house, saw the same Mr. John sitting in a chair at his fire-side; and, being astonished to find him there, told what he had seen, of which the minister did not seem to take much notice; but thereafter, in three or four days, desired to know of him the circumstances of what he had seen; and the young man insisting that he saw him come out of the house the moment he entered, he said, the scene appears to be intended for a warning, but enjoined my informer to conceal it from his spouse. He died the same year, according to this and other presages of his approaching end.

On occasions, we can date a dream or vision accurately due to the circumstances surrounding it. Such is the case in this next example recorded by Theophilus Insulanus. The date was Saturday, 25th of October 1760. He writes:

> John Macleod, tacksman of Bay in the Isle of Sky, a gentleman not in the least tinctured with enthusiasm, declared to me, and several others, that, in a morning before he awaked, he dreamed, that a person whom he intimately knew came into the room where he lay, and told him, with much concern, that his late Majesty, George the Second of glorious memory, was departed this life, which he told directly to his spouse in bed with him; that same day the post having come on before he had well dressed, he got the public news, in which he found his dream verified which is the more remarkable, that the King's death was so sudden, the account of his ailment could not have travelled to many parts in England, much less have time to circulate to the most remote parts of Scotland.

Leaving the island for a moment and moving firstly to Loch Broom on the North West coast, we have three very interesting accounts, recorded by 'Lord Tarbut', George Mackenzie, 1st Earl of Cromarty (1630-1714). The first of these involves a sceptic.

In the year 1653, Alexander Munro (afterwards Lieutenant-Colonel to the Earl of Dumbarton's regiment) and I was walking in a place called ... (a blank space in the M.S.), in Loch Broom, in a little plain at the foot of a rugged hill; there was a servant working with a spade in the walk before us, his back to us, and his face to the hill. He took no notice of us, though we passed by near to him, which made me look at him, and perceiving that he stared I conjectured he was a Seer; wherefore I called to him, at which he started and smiled. 'What are you doing?' said I; he answered, 'I have seen a very strange thing - an army of Englishmen, leading of horses, coming down that hill; and a number of them are come down to the plain, and eating the barley which is growing in the field near to the hill.' This was the 4th of May (for I noted the day), and it was four or five days before the barley was sown in the field he spoke of. Alexander Munro asked him how he knew they were Englishmen; he answered 'Because they were leading horses, and had hats and boots, which he knew no Scotchman would have on there.' We took little notice of the whole story as other than a foolish vision, but wished that an English party were there, we being at war with them, and the place almost inaccessible for horsemen. But the beginning of August thereafter, the Earl of Middleton, then Lieutenant for the King in the Highlands, having occasion to march a party of his towards the South Islands, sent his foot through a place called Inverlaewell, and the forepart, which was first down the hill, did fall to eating the barley which was on the little plain under it, and Munro, calling to mind what the Seer told us in May preceding, wrote of it, and sent an express to me to Lochslime in Ross (where I then was) with it.

I had occasion to be in company where a young lady was (excuse my not naming of persons), and I was told that there was a notable Seer in company, and I called to him to speak with me, and after he had answered several questions, I asked him if he saw any person to be in love with that lady. He said he did, but knew not the person, for during the two days he had been in her company, he perceived one standing near her with his head leaning on her shoulder, which he said did foretell that the man should marry her, and die before her, according to his observation. This was in the year 1655. I desired him to describe the person, which he did; so I could conjecture by the description that it was such a one who was of that lady's acquaintance, though there was no thought of their intermarriage till two years later; and having occasion in the year 1657 to find this Seer, who was an Islander, in company with the other person whom I conjectured to have been described by him, I called him aside, and asked him if that was the person he saw beside the lady near two years then past. He said it was he indeed, for he had seen that lady just then standing by him hand-in-hand. This was some few months before their marriage, and the man is since dead, and the lady is still alive.

I shall trouble you with but one more, which I thought the most remarkable of all that occurred to me. In Jan., 1682, the above named Colonel Munro and I happened to be in the house of William Macleod, of Fierinhed, in the county of Ross; he, the landlord, and I sitting on three chairs near the fire, and in the corner of the great chimney there were two Islanders, who were that very night come to the house, and were related to the landlord. While one of them was talking with Munro, I perceived the other to look oddly towards me, and from his looks, and his being an Islander, I conjectured that he was a Seer, and asked him why he stared? He answered by desiring me to rise from the chair, for it was an unlucky one. I asked 'Why ?' He answered, 'Because, there was a dead man in the chair next to it.' 'Well,' said I, 'If it be but in the next, I may safely sit here; but what is the likeness of the man?' He said he was a tall man with a long grey coat, booted, and one of his legs hanging over the chair, and his head hanging down to the other side, and his arm backward as if it were broken. There were some English troops quartered near the place, and there being at that time a great frost after a thaw, the country was wholly covered with ice. Four or five Englishmen riding by this house, not two hours after the vision, where we were sitting by the fire, we heard a great noise, which proved to be these troopers, with the help of other servants, carrying in one of their number who got a very mischievous fall, and his arm broken ; and falling frequently into swooning fits, they brought him into the hall, and set him in the very chair and in the very posture which the Seer had proposed ; but the man did not die, though he revived with great difficulty.[1]

ENDNOTE

1. Norman MacRae & Rev. Wm. Morrison, *Highland Second Sight*, (George Souter, Dingwall.) c1908, pp. 61-64.

CHAPTER 6

Doubt & Hostility

I am surprised that people professing Christianity, will believe nothing but what is comprehended by our vitiated reason and weak judgment; this argues the height of pride or ignorance.

Malcolm MacAskill, minister of the Small Islands (1763)

The above statement is part of a reply written on July 29, 1763, by Malcolm MacAaskill in response to a letter from Theophilus Insulanus. From the tone of his reply, it becomes clear that not everyone to whom MacLeod had written seeking material for his book was sympathetic to his point of view. Indeed MacAskill is quite scathing of the naysayers:

> I am just taking my boat for the Small Isles, and have no time on hand; whenever I arrive in my dominions, I intend to go to Arisaig. I wish, from the bottom of my heart, that some of my cloth would carry themselves with more decency towards their superiors in most branches of literature, and call to mind that they are only sacred while in the pulpit. But the plain truth is, to tell it to my friend H-r, as they cannot come

up to your towering genius, they endeavour to pull down your well connected scheme. Go on and prosper, amidst the sneers and ill-nature of parsons and factors. Let U-h study his droving, and may he grope all his days about the tails of his cows and stots, as his genius leads that way, and was born for no higher lucubrations. Let your P—n examine his bible, and if he peruses it with attention, unless he has put on the firmest resolution of remaining an infidel, I should have rather said an apostate, he must cry Peccavi.[1] I am in hurry. Rundonnan, his wife, and mine, offer their most unfeigned and sincerest compliments to Mr. MacLeod, Miss Mally, and the common friend of mankind, H—r; and believe me to be, dear Sir, your much obliged, and most humble servant. Malcolm MacAskill. Rundonnan (Rubha an Dùnain2), July 29, 1736.

Malcolm MacAskill was born in 1723 and was the son 'M. of Rhuandunan', Isle of Skye. He was educated at the University of Edinburgh. His first charge was as a minister in the parish of Kilmallie. He was subsequently transferred to the parish of the Small Isles in 1757. He was married twice, firstly, to Ann MacLeod, daughter of one Murdoch MacLeod from Glenelg. Malcolm and Ann had three children - Kenneth, John and Jean. Of these three, only Jean survived to adulthood, living in Rudha an Dunain, Isle of Skye. His second wife, whom he married on 21st July 1761, was 'Mairi Nighean Eoghain', (Mary MacLean) daughter of Hugh MacLean XIV of Coll. Malcolm and Mary had 10 children one of whom was Donald, (b 1763) who became a Medical Doctor. Tragically he drowned crossing from Arisaig to Eigg on the 28th of October 1817.

When MacAskill initially arrived in Eigg and his glebe was extended, it is said he invited a relative, John MacAskill, (b.1727 in Minginish, Skye), to come to Eigg to help him. John MacAskill was known as Iain Mòr, and is listed in the 1764 census of the Small Isles as 'Church Elder', along with his wife Marion Cumming, (b.1728) and four children as well as Marion Cameron, a widow, aged 76. Malcolm MacAskill was reputed to have been a man of 'splendid physique and great strength; was called Am Ministear Laidir (The strong minister) and wore a shepherd tartan kilt.' Interestingly, the founders of Talisker Distillery, Ewen and Allan MacAskill, were grandsons of the Rev. Malcolm MacAskill.

A letter dated 30th April 1736, from 'MacLeod of Hamar - Theophilus Insulanus - Skye', had also been received by 'Normand Morison' at Balnakil, Uig, Isle of Lewis on the 9th May 1763. In reply Morison states that he will subscribe for a bound copy of Hamar's *Treatise on Second Sight*, then about to be published, but he assures MacLeod that no one in the parish could read but himself.

Morison was the third known minister in Uig, Lewis (1742-1777). He is said to have been a grandson of John Morison, Tacksman at Bragar, known apparently as the 'Indweller of Bragar'. His father was Rev. John Morison, of Urray. Normand (Norman) Morison studied at Aberdeen and St Andrews and from his ordination in 1742, spent his whole working life in Uig, Lewis. His church is said to have been 'a small blackhouse just outside the present Baile na Cille walled garden, near the cemetery.' Interestingly, Morison was a brother of John Morison 'The Petty Seer' (mentioned earlier) minister of Petty (near Inverness) from 1759 to 1774. Little is known of the life of Norman Morison or his experience of the supernatural. However the historian Murdo Macaulay has left us one incident of interest:

> On a certain occasion in harvest-time Mr Morison went to Great Bernera to preach. The turn-out on Sunday was so meagre that he felt quite discouraged. His displeasure at this indifference became clear when he was engaged in prayer. He addressed the West wind as follows: "Duisg thusa O'ghaoth ghlolach an Iar, agus seid agus duisgas an cadal-sabaid na paganaich nach duisg gu eisdeachd ris an fhuaim aoibhneach." - "Awake O hollow West-wind, and blow and rouse up the pagans out of their Sabbath slumbers, who will not wake to hear the joyful sound." It is said that the West wind did blow, and blow such a hurricane that it was remembered for long on account of the damage it did to their corn.[3]

If some were opposed - there were, even among those who were open to such things, times when they appear to have been unsure as to how to deal with certain phenomena and had themselves to question its source of origin. Such was the case in one incident involving Rev. John Fraser (c1647-1702) whom we have already quoted extensively:

> I Remember about twenty three years ago, there was an Old Woman in my Parish in the Isle of Tirey, whom I heard was accustomed to give Responses, and likewise averred that she had Died and been in Heaven, but allowed to come back again; and because she could not come to Church, I was at the pains to give her a Visit, attended with two or three of the most intelligent of my Parish: I questioned her first, whither she said she was in Heaven, And she freely confessed she was, and that she had seen Jesus Christ, but not God the Father or the Holy Ghost; that she was kindly entertained with Meat and Drink, and that she had seen her Daughter there, who Died about a year before, that her Daughter told her though she was allowed to goe there, that she behooved to come back and serve out her Prentiship on Earth, but would shortly be called for, and remain there for ever. She could very hardly be put out of this Opinion till I enquired, more narrowly of her Children, if she fell at any time in a Syncopa, which they told me she did, and continued for a whole night, so that they thought that she was truly Dead, and this is the time she alleaged she was in Heaven; The Devil took an advantage in the Ecstasy, to present to her fancy a Map of Heaven as if it had been a Rich Earthly Kingdom, abounding with Meat, Drink, Gold, and Silver; By the Blessing of God, I prevailed with her to be persuaded that this was but a Vision presented to her fancy by the Devil, the Father of Lies; and that she might deprehend the falshood of it from this one head, that she imagined her Body was there, as well as her Soul, and that she did Eat and Drink and was Warmed, while as her own Children and the Neighbours that watched her, did see, and did handle her Body several times that night, so that it could not be with her in Heaven. I did further examin her what warrand she had for the Responses she gave, which were found very often true, even in future contingent events: she freely confessed that her Father upon his Death-Bed

taught her a Charm compiled of Barbarous words, and some unteligible terms, which had the Vertue when repeated, to present some few hours after the proposition of a question the answer of the same, in live Images before her Eyes, or upon the Wall, but the Images were not tractable, which she found by putting to her hand, but could find nothing. I do not think fit to insert the charm, knowing that severals might be Inclined to make an unwarrantable tryal of it. This Poor Woman was got reclaimed, and was taught fully the danger and vanity of her practice, and died peaceably about a year after, in extreme old Age.[4]

Another person with whom Theophilus Insulanus corresponded was the Rev. Martin MacPherson, minister of Golspie. Interestingly, MacPherson does not hold out hope of being able to furnish him with much information. He writes:

I am sorry to observe, that it will not be in my power to procure many subscribers. The act of the British Parliament against putting witches to death, or torture, was owing to one of these good women, who was burnt in the soles, and hanged in this place, about thirty or odd years ago; and you can not imagine what influence that act of the British Senate has had on the minds of the people, who have drawn conclusions from it, that were never supposed by the law-makers: those particularly among us, that should be the of men encouragers and works of merit, seem to admire the wisdom of the houses of Parliament, in this instance, at least, as much as the sacred oracles themselves, and have wisely inferred from this act, that there is no such thing as a communication, or agency of spirits on our minds or senses.

The case MacPherson was probably referring to was that of Janet Horne, an old lady with a daughter and a husband. She was disabled and possibly senile when she was accused and convicted of being a witch. The final nail in her coffin was mispronouncing one word in the Lord's Prayer when asked to repeat it! She was burnt to death in Dornoch in 1727, the last person in the UK to be so. Little wonder few in Sutherland wanted to speak about their experiences of the supernatural.

Historian Douglas Ansdell has noted:

> The Presbyterian churches in the Highlands were committed to the eradication of all forms of magic and superstition in the parish. There was, however, a measure of uncertainty about some supernatural events, such as second sight, visions and miracles. The ability to foretell future events has been both shunned and applauded by the Highland church. It had been excluded as an unacceptable aspect of a superstitious society and welcomed as a spiritual gift. There are many accounts of ministers and church members foretelling deaths, predicting what text a minister would preach from, having foreknowledge of people in trouble and of visitors whose arrival was imminent. Mr Lachlan MacKenzie, minister of Lochcarron, was one to whom this ability was attributed. He once announced there are 'five young men present here today that shall be in eternity before this day, six weeks, and none of them above twenty-eight years of age.' This came true. John Kennedy, minister of Dingwall, provided a Christian rationale for second sight by describing it as the secret of the Lord.'[5]

We have seen previously that Theophilus Insulanus recorded of 'Reverend Mr. Donald MacLeod' it was 'as if he had believed that revelation by dreams and visions was entirely ceased' – so also do many today within religious circles – especially so among the group identified as 'Conservative Evangelicals'. In addition to incredulity and doubt it was and is also the fear that the issues we have been examining originate in the realms of darkness and were/are consequently 'sinful' and to be avoided at all costs. Theophilus Insulanus records such an instance that occurred in the Isle of Lewis:

> A woman of Stornbay (Stornoway) in Lewis had a maid who saw visions, and often fell into a swoon; her

mistress was very much concerned about her, but could not find out any means to prevent her seeing those things at last she resolved to pour some of the water used in baptism on her maid's face, believing this would prevent her seeing any more sights of this kind. And accordingly she carried her maid with her next Lord's day, and both of them sat near the basin in which the water stood, and after baptism before the minister had concluded the last prayer, she put her hand in the bason, took up as much water as she could, and threw it on the maid's face; at which strange action the minister and the congregation were equally surprised. After prayer, the minister inquired of the woman the meaning of such an unbecoming and distracted action; she told him, it was to prevent her maid's seeing visions: and it fell out accordingly, for from that time she never once more saw a vision of any kind.

That others were and are troubled by their experience of dreams, premonitions and visions is obvious from the available evidence. Martin Martin records the following story:

John Morison, who lives in Bernera of Harries, wears the plant called Fuga Damonum,[6] sewed in the neck of his coat, to prevent his seeing of visions, and says he never saw any since he first carried that plant about him. He suffered me to feel the plant in the neck of his coat, but would by no means let me open the seam, though I offered him a reward to let me do it.

In her book *Father Allan's Island* (1920), Amy Murray records similar reticence among some in relation to Second Sight on the strongly Roman Catholic Hebridean Island of Erisky:

And here's a young girl beginning the same way. She saw a vision, so her sister opened and shut the Bible before her face, that the wind might blow in her eyes. Since then she does not see, but she can hear and feel the creak of the stakes, the breath of the bearers on her cheek, and their feet stumbling over hers on the path of a dark night, when the wraith of a funeral-to-be goes by her.

Interestingly, the subject of this book was himself credited with having the gift of Second Sight. Father Allan MacDonald (1859 - 1905) who served as Roman Catholic Priest on the Island of Eriskay recorded stories relating to his own experiences of Second Sight as well as those of others from Eriskay and the Uist's. These can be found in the book *Strange Things* (1968) by John L. Campbell and Trevor H. Hall.

Walking on Eriskay one day with MacDonald, Murray heard him calling out to 'a man delving his potato-patch, "What weather will we have?" "We call him "the prophet," he added in my ear. "Seven days of sunshine," gave back "the prophet" promptly, whereat we laughed. Seven days of sunshine nevertheless we had.'

Theophilus Insulanus himself has left a clear record of his own view concering the veracity of these things:

> It will not seem strange, that deists and free thinkers, who deny all revelation, should at the same time declare their reluctance to believe apparitions, and to raise what dust they can to cloud and discredit it; as they are sensible their yielding this point, would be urged against them with great propriety, to overthrow their false system of faith; but it is much more surprising, and indeed lamentable that Christians, who profess to believe the Sacred Oracles as they are handed down to us in the Scriptures of the Old and New Testament, should discover any scruple to admit the truth of apparitions; which so powerfully prompt and en force the important belief of revelation: yet after all they can say, what does their opinion amount to in point of argument? If a few singular and extravagant persons are extremely confident, that a thing does not exist, is that a proof against experience that it does really exist? Such as have this unhappy cast of mind, will please read over (a list of proof text follows) … particularly Joel 2: 28 -

And it shall come to pass afterward, that I will pour out my spirit upon all flesh, and your sons and your daughters shall prophesy, your old men shall dream dreams, your young men shall see visions. And also upon the servants and upon the handmaids in those days, will I pour out my spirit. These, of many that might be added from the word of God, I presume, is sufficient to confirm those Christians, who find themselves squeamish to believe apparitions.

In another place, Theophilus records a very unusual story and adds his own opinion once again:

About forty years ago, one Mr. Alexander Cunnison, Minister of the gospel on the island of Mull, being visited late at night by a neighbouring gentleman, who was followed by a large greyhound, they took supper; but after they had gone to bed, the greyhound quarrelled with the house-cat, and soon despatched it; he then attacked a maid-servant, who giving the cry, the minister came to rescue her, but unfortunately was wounded in several parts in the fray; which his wife observing, both she and her sister, (a young maid in the house,) came to the minister's assistance, and, in the scuffle, received wounds, having, with much ado, turned out the mad dog: he entered a cottage or two hard by, where he destroyed three persons : all that he had bit died in the greatest disorder; only Mr. Cunnison caused himself to be bled to death. Mr. John Cunnison his father, being also a minister, and living in Kintyre, had a revelation of the above melancholy scene, and told his wife and all the family, that, upon that very night, his son, with his wife and severals of his family, had suffered a violent death, exhorting his spouse to patience, and a resignation to the will of God, that she might be prepared to receive those tidings, which ere long would spread, and come to her ears from all quarters. One Duncan Campbell, (who lived a door neighbour to me in former for two years, declared to him frequently, that he lived with Mr. John Cunnison, a servant at the time, and was in the house the same night when he told the whole family (and himself among the rest) the tragical end of his son and others that suffered on the same occasion.

One would think it scarce possible, that a deist or free-thinker, who peruseth these instances, with others of the same stamp, (of which the Jewish, Christian, and Heathen history are full,) should be able to impose on themselves so much as to deny the truth of apparitions; but it is to be feared, while any remain of the species, one or other (without the immediate interposition of Providence) will be so governed by prejudice and rampant lusts, as to fly in the face of the most glaring evidence. It is very remarkable, and claims our utmost attention, that those intimations we receive in dreams, and by the Second Sight, or apparitions, are chiefly employed to forewarn us of the approaching end of some relations, neighbours, or acquaintances.

One minister who would later fall in to the category spoken of by Theophilus was the Rev. Alexander Beith (1799-1891). It happened that one night (c1830-37) Beith was staying in the home of Isaac Lillingston at Balmacara House, near Kyle of Lochalsh. Given that these events are recounted by a sceptic they are all the more authentic. Beith himself takes up story:

> I retired to my bedroom before midnight. It was a large attic room at the east end of the house - an attic so large, that four beds were placed in it, one at each of the four corners. The door was directly opposite to the fireplace, which prepared for me, on the night in question, was to the left of the fireplace, the foot of the bed being towards the fire, which was shaded off, and out of sight, by the thick bed-curtain. The door was in full view of the bed, to the left. None of the other beds was occupied. No one slept that night in the main body of the house (the servants' apartments were in the two wings) except Mr. and Mrs. Lillingston, and myself. Their bedroom was situated on the ground floor. The drawing room floor intervened between it and the attic which I occupied.

I had gone to bed. After a little, I fell asleep, and I slept I know not how long. Suddenly I was awakened by what I imagined was a loud knock at my door. I opened my eyes: the fire was still burning but was about to expire. I called, "Come in". No sooner had I done so than I saw the door slowly open. A man of gigantic stature, of huge proportions, red-haired, half-dressed, his brawny arms bare high above the elbows, presented himself to my view. I saw him distinctly advance, not towards me, but direct to the fireplace, the glimmering light from the grate falling on his massive frame. He carried a large black chest, which appeared to me to be studded with brass nails, and to be so heavy as to tax to the utmost his strength, stalwart figure as he was. I saw him pass the foot of my bed, as if turning to the side of the fire next the bed towards the opposite angle of the room, on the same line. The black chest seemed to grow into a coffin of dread dimensions. In that form I saw it but for a moment. My bed-curtain almost instantly concealed from my eyes the bearer and his burden. He set it down with a crash which startled me, as I thought, and which seemed to shake the house, and, as I believed, fairly aroused me. I tried to look round to the fireplace, but I saw nothing. Everything was as I had left it on going into bed. The vision had passed. In whatever condition I had been previously, I felt confident I was, by that time, thoroughly awake.

Reflecting on the incident, I soon set the whole affair down to a fit of nightmare, brought on, perhaps, by the conversation in which I had been so deeply interested before retiring to rest, and which had somewhat excited my nervous system. In a short time I had got over my agitation, and was composing myself to sleep, when I again suddenly heard a knock at my door. I raised myself on my elbow, with a resolution to be at the bottom of it, and said firmly, perhaps fiercely, "Come in". The door opened, when Mr Lillingston appeared, in his dressing gown, a light in his hand. As he was in figure tall, though not robust, and of a reddish complexion, his appearance slightly resembled what I had previously seen. "Have you been ill?" "No; I am quite well". " Have you been out of bed?", "No" I certainly have not, since I lay down". "Mrs. Lillingston and I have been disturbed by hearing heavy steps in your room, as we thought, and by the sound of the falling of some weighty article on the floor. There must have been some mistake". He bade me goodnight, withdrew, and left me to my reflections.

Sleep came towards morning. At breakfast, when we all met there, the noise which had been heard became the subject of conversation. I made no mention of the vision; that I kept to myself. I suggested that something might have fallen directly overhead in the drawing room. We went and examined it, but nothing could be seen; all the furniture stood, every part of it, in its wonted place. Had we been able to explain the noise there would have been nothing in the occurrence that might be accounted uncommon. Even with that unexplained (the giving or yielding, of some joint in a piece of furniture might have done it), there was nothing very unusual in what had occurred.

I would have forgotten it altogether, but the succession of deaths in our family just a year after-four children, as already noted, being taken from us within a few weeks- brought up the remembrance of what I had seen, and I felt a strange - an unreasonable inclination I am willing to admit - to connect the two things, and to conclude that what I had witnessed, or imagined I had witnessed, in the Balmacara attic, was a kindly presentiment or pre-intimation of sorrow to come. It had some effect in making my heart, and another heart too, tender, in anticipating trial which might overtake us, for which we felt it became us to stand prepared - trial of a kind that we had not, at that time, ever tasted.[7]

A short time after this experience, when Beith was minister in Glenelg, tragedy struck his family. Four of his children died over a period of some of six weeks.

With Beith and his experience comes a break in the continuum of the era we have been looking at so far. From the beginning of the nineteenth century various Evangelical movements, identified as 'Revivals' of Awakenings' began to have a strong influence and impact spiritually and socially as well as religiously in Skye and the Hebrides. Records of revelations, premonitions, visions and dreams, which were once so widespread in society in general, are now replaced by recorded experiences within this new religious atmosphere. To these we will turn in our next chapter.

ENDNOTES

1. 'Peccavi' - an admission of guilt or responsibility, or an acknowledgemen of sin.

2. In the post-Viking era Rubha an Dùnain was the hereditary homeland of the clan MacAskill, a sept of Clan McLeod, for whom they were coast-watchers and bodyguards. The peninsula contains the ruins of a farming community, including an 18th-century Tacksman's house. At its zenith during the early years of the 19th century, the Rubha an Dùnain farm extended to 37,500 acres (15,200 hectares) and directly supported 70 men and scores of families. The area was occupied until the clearances. (Wikipedia)

3. Rev. Murdo MacAulay, *Aspects of the Religious History of Lewis Up to the Disruption of 1843* (John G. Eccles printers Ltd, Inverness) c1986 pp. 103-104.

4. Rev, John Fraser, *Deuteroskopia or a Brief Discourse concerning the Second Sight, commonly so called* (1754 edition) p.9.

5. Douglas Ansdell, *The People of the Great Faith* (Acair Limited, 7 James Street, Stornoway, Scotland) 1998 pp.134-135.

6. St John's wort is a deeply metaphysical plant. Known in the middle ages as Fuga daemonum, or Scare Devil, even its botanical name – Hypericum perforatum – gives a clue to its occult past. Derived from the Greek words hyper (meaning "over") and eikon ("apparition"), it provides a further reminder that the herb was used to vanquish evil spirits and ghosts. (The Guardian, Lifestyle, 21st March 2002)

7. Alexander Beith, *A Highland Tour,* (Edinburgh: Adam and Charles Black, 1874), pp.84-88.

CHAPTER 7

The New Seers

Oh if you saw the camp (of Angels) *surrounding Dr. Kennedy!*

James Mathieson (1805-1875)

With the coming of Evangelicalism to Skye and the Hebrides – so also did a new experience of the supernatural. Prior to this movement, the people of the Islands and Highlands appear, for various reasons, to have been thoroughly fed up with traditional religion, so much so that when this spiritual tsunami broke on the shores of Skye and the other Hebridean Islands the national church, the Church of Scotland, was, to a greater or lesser extent, abandoned. The first spiritual storm made landfall on Skye between 1812 and 1814 – and was fermented primarily by one man, a blind fiddler – Donald Munro. Although active throughout the Island, it appears Donald was initially most active in the Kilmuir area – and it was here that one of the first groups (referred to by opponents as a 'sect') outside the establishment, was set up. Interestingly, it was led by a 'prophetess'. Her name was Flora McPherson.

Writing for the May 1817 issue of the *Edinburgh Christian Instructor*, the Rev. Donald Ross, Kilmuir, (an arch-enemy of Donald Munro) was scathing of McPherson and her followers. Regrettably, his appears to be the only surviving account of this woman and the church she led. He noted that the group was,

> Headed up by a poor illiterate woman named Flora McPherson, commonly known by the name the Prophetess. Her errors were embraced by a considerable number of the people - her wildest reveries were looked upon as divine illuminations; some of the most serious and best disposed were seduced by her imposing appearance, and viewing her in the light of one inspired, the people considered it incumbent upon them to place the most unbounded confidence in everything that dropped from the lips of one whom they believed gifted with supernatural endowments. The distinguishing traits of her character were roaring, violent convulsions, high pretensions to inspiration, and communication with the Saviour.

However, Ross was also forced to concede that,

> Some of both sexes who were before of abandoned lives, came at that time under serious impressions of religion which have ever remained undefaced; and to this day they continue patterns of piety, zeal, and devotedness to God.[1]

The opposition of most clergy to this and subsequent such movements, especially on Skye, resulted in a dearth of reliable written testimony regarding its early progress, phenomena and the experiences associated with it. What we do know is that it was accompanied by great emotion, prostrations and visions – but sadly, little has been recorded, and much of what has come from opponents and naysayers. That is not to say we cannot find a thread linking the old spirituality with the new – and as time went on more information was forthcoming. As this movement began to mature during the years which followed and especially after the rupture of the national Church and the formation of the Free Church of Scotland in 1843 – much more evidence began to emerge as to the shape of the new spirituality and the experiences of the dreams, visions and premonitions of the Seers and Prophets who were now active within it. But to understand all this we must pause and leave the shores of Skye for a moment in order to see the place of the prophetic within the experience of earlier religious groups and individuals in the Highlands in general.

Donald Roy - Nigg, Ross-shire.

Hugh Miller of Cromarty (Scottish geologist, writer and folklorist) wrote – 'Neither Peden nor Cargill, nor any of the other prophets of the covenant, were favoured with clearer revelations of the future than some of the Highland seers'. One of the men Miller was referring to was Donald Roy, who lived in Nigg, Easter Ross. Donald, one of the area's best shinty players, was converted to Christianity as a young man and was subsequently made an elder in the Presbyterian Church shortly after the revolution settlement of 1689 – 90.

Miller described Roy as – 'Belonging to that extraordinary class of men who, (lived) as it were, on the extreme verge of the natural world, and (saw) far in to the world of spirits.'

On one occasion when he was about 90 years old, Donald was working with two other men at Castle-Craig farm. Due to a heavy snowstorm during the afternoon, the men retired to a barn. As Donald's two companions were speaking to each other they noted Donald sitting at the other end of the barn, his eyes fixed on the wall. As they observed, Donald would raise his arms and then clasp his hands as if he were witnessing some terrible scene. They then heard him muttering to himself and as they listened heard him say – 'Let her drive – let her drive! – Dinna haud her side to the sea.' Then striking his hands together, he shouted out – 'She's o'er

– She's o'er – Oh the puir widows o' Dunskaith! – but God's will be done'. 'Elder', said one of the men, 'are ye no weel? – ya wald better gang in till the house'. 'No' said Donald, 'let's awa to the burn o' Nigg, there has been ill enough come o' this sad night already – let's awa to the burn, or there'll be more. Leaving the barn the three men went out in the storm and hurried a considerable distance to the burn where they found a poor woman who had collapsed from exhaustion in the snow a few minutes before they had arrived. She was carried to the nearest cottage and soon recovered. The next morning the darker vision was confirmed when the wreck of a Dunskaith boat and the bodies of some of the crew were found on the beach below Craig.

On another occasion Donald's 30 year old granddaughter, who lived some distance away, contracted a dangerous fever and her life was in danger. This occurred unknown to Donald. However the woman's husband, who was passing through Nigg, called on him and brought him the sad news. 'Step in on your coming back' said Donald 'and dinna tine heart – for she's in gude hands'. Three hours later the man returned and Donald came out to meet him at the door. 'Come in Robert', he said, 'and cool yoursel, ye hae travelled ower hard – come in, and dinna be sae distressed, for there's nae cause. Kettie will get o'er this, and live to see the youngest o' her bairins settled in the world, and doing for themselves'. On his return home the man found that the fever had left his wife and she was on her feet within a short time. She lived to fulfil the prophecy of her grandfather. Donald Roy died in 1774 aged 109.

Rev. John Porteous, Kilmuir-Easter, Ross-shire.

A striking example of prophetic insight can be found in the experience of the Rev. John Porteous, Kilmuir-Easter, Ross-shire, (1704 - 1775). On one occasion the Earl of Cromarty sent for John in order to belittle him over a certain matter. John Porteous replied with dignity and with what proved prophetic accuracy,

You have sent for me to insult me; the time is not remote when I can enter at this door and pass through all the apartments in your castle, and go out where I please, and you will not dare to come near it. It will no longer be an abode for human beings, but for the fowls of heaven. As a proof of this thorns will grow where I now stand.

The Earl scoffed, but, despite his mocking, the words were soon fulfilled. It is a matter of historical record that as a result of the Earl attaching himself to the supporters of the 1745 rebellion, he was sentenced to life imprisonment, and his former castle fell in to ruins.

Lachlan MacKenzie, Lochcarron, Ross-shire.

The famed Rev. Lachlan MacKenzie of Lochcarron (1754-1819) was, as we have already seen, also revered as a Prophet. Donald MacLean, himself a native of Lochcarron wrote – 'That he uttered predictions is as unquestionably true as that some of them had startling fulfilment'. It is said that Eneas Sage a previous minister at Lochcarron was also revered as a Prophet. Sage denied that he possessed the prophetic gift. However, Lachlan MacKenzie is not known to have made such a denial. MacKenzie prophesied that, as a sign of the validity of the faith he preached, following his death, two trees, of a variety, hitherto alien to Lochcarron, would grow up on either side of the pulpit from which he preached. He further stated that when these trees grew their branches would become entwined and the trees eventually fall to the ground as a sign that the apostasy of the latter day had begun! All this did in fact occur after his death. In 1930 it was reported of the trees – 'They fell over on the ground where they lie in a decaying condition, but still there'. Shortly before his death, Lachlan prophesied that his successor would be 'a dumb dog that would not bark'. This too was proved correct – in the spiritual sense!

Rev. John Morrison, Petty, Inverness.

Morrison was, perhaps, the best-known of the Highland prophets of the eighteenth century. He was born in 1701 in the parish of Dull, Perthshire and became the Parish Minister of Petty, between Inverness and Nairn, in 1759. Reminiscences of his life, times and many of his prophetic statements are contained in the little booklet (undated) by A.B. MacLennan – entitled – *The Petty Seer*. Writing in *Times of Blessing* in 1876, Donald Corbet, Free Church Minister of Kinlochbervie, noted of both Morrison and his father:

> 'Their theological knowledge was minute and extensive; and their success in the ministry, both in the conversion of sinners and in the edification of the household of faith, was, I may say, extraordinary … After his settlement in Petty, his church was day after day literally crammed to the door with crowds hungering for the Bread of Life. That continued to the termination of his course.'

On one occasion John Morrison was on his way from Petty to Inverness to officiate at a communion, accompanied by his servant. As they approached Milton of Culloden, the road was crowded with people on their way to the Sacrament. 'You see the large number of people there', observed the minister, 'yet only six of them will go to heaven. As a proof that I know the truth of what I say, the innkeeper there (pointing to the inn which was then near the road at Milton), who is now in good health, will be in eternity before you return to Inverness.' On his return journey, the servant boy enquired for the innkeeper at Milton, to be told that he had fallen down the stairs while drunk, a short time before, and had broken his neck.

A number of Morrison's prophetic statements, and the fulfilment of them, were highly unusual. Preaching in his own church on one occasion Morrison predicted that a large rock, known as 'Clach dubh an Adain', and which marked the boundary between the estates of Lord Murray and Culloden, would be carried seaward without any human intervention. Some 26 years later, on the 20th of February 1799, the rock, which weighed at least eight tons, was carried 260 yards out to sea. The only explanation available was that a large sheet of ice had formed under the rock and that a hurricane, on the rising tide, had blown it out to sea.

James Matheson, Dornoch, Sutherland.

Another man who lived, on the extreme edge of the natural world, and saw far into the world of spirits, was James Matheson (1805 -1875). James was born and lived at Clashnagarve, which lies about five miles northwest of Dornoch. Adopting Christianity as a young man, James Matheson was, it is said, pre-eminently a man of deep devotion and prayer. One indication of the esteem in which he was held was seen when, on one occasion, he dined with the renowned Rev. Dr John Kennedy in the Dornoch Church manse. After the meal James rose to pray and the minister went down on his knees at his feet.

Beside the burn which ran near his home was a hollow where James spent many hours in prayer. For many years after his death, the mark of his knees could be seen in the ground. On one occasion James and a friend attended a communion at Creich, where Dr. Kennedy was preaching to thousands on the hillside. After a short time, his friend observed that James's face was shining in an unusual way. The friend enquired as to the reason for his obvious delight, to which James replied – 'Oh if you saw the camp surrounding Dr. Kennedy!' Although the friend could see nothing, James was transfixed by the sight of the angelic host surrounding the preacher. Nor was this the only time James experienced such a view of the unseen world.

During the Crimean War James rarely if ever slept in his bed – spending extraordinary periods in prayer. Some men from the 93rd Highlanders fighting in the trenches, saw, on more than one occasion, a strange man moving about the trenches. After returning home at the end of the war, some of these men were at a communion in Creich, when, for the first time, they saw James. They recognised him as the man who had appeared to them in Crimea!

But as we move on from the times of these earlier religious Seers to the days of Donald Munro, Flora McPherson and others - we discover that many who kept the flame of the prophetic alive were, like Flora, women. And while Skye seems to fade in to the background somewhat at this point in relation to these gifts, at least in the recording of them, its sister island to the north, Lewis and Harris would, to a greater or lessor extent, take centre stage.

ENDNOTE

1. *The Edinburgh Christian Instructor,* May 1817, p.286. (Document held by the National Library of Scotland, Edinburgh.)

CHAPTER 8

The Prophetic Women of Lewis

By the time you receive this, I will be in Glory and you won't be long after me.

John MacKay (c1870)

As a result of the waves of spiritual renewal in the Hebrides in the mid to late nineteenth century there emerged a deep prophetic spirituality among the people. Prominent among these were women from the Isle of Lewis and Harris – and to a few of these we now turn.[1]

Catherine Mackay (Catriona Hangie)

Catriona was born in Bavas on the Isle of Lewis in 1789. She was described by the Rev. Alisdair MacRae as being 'Tall and handsome in her bearing with a face that radiated spiritual beauty.' She wrote and sang her own Gaelic hymns.

Catriona's life was difficult in the extreme. When her father died she had no right to the land he crofted and the landowner denied her the use of the field to plant crops. One day she was pulling up old potato plants in an attempt to find something from last year's crop. Seeing her the landowner attacked her – pushing her face into the ground. As she rose she told him his days were numbered and that his horses, which were grazing nearby, would soon carry his remains to the nearby cemetery. It was not long before her prophetic words were fulfilled.

One of her friends, a John Mackay from Barvas, had been treated similarly by the landowner – and had been forced to emigrate to Canada. On the day he died, Catriona said – 'My loved one has no need of my prayers tonight.' Later a letter arrived from him which said – 'By the time you receive this, I will be in Glory and you won't be long after me.' Catriona died on a Sunday morning in the year 1871.

Gormelia MacLean (Goramal 'An Fhivig)

Gormelia was born in the small township of Fhivig near Shawbost on the Isle of Lewis. Like Catriona Hangie, Gormelia lived a life of poverty and constant dependence on God.

One day, as a young girl, while she was working on the seashore with some other women she suddenly left and set off for the nearby village of Bragar. On arrival she entered the home of an elderly Christian, Malcolm Campbell. Malcom and a friend had in fact been praying for someone to come and help them. That day Malcolm had been given a silver half-crown and was convinced that the money was for someone else. However, with no transport, they were unable to travel and pass to coin on. Gormelia was the answer to their prayers! She received her instructions and took the coin to a dying woman who was praying that God would not allow her to die till her outstanding debt to the local shopkeeper had been paid.

Margaret (MacIver) MacKenzie (Cailleach Tob)

Margaret was born in the village of Cross, Ness on the Isle of Lewis in 1870. While she was still very young she had a strange dream which made a deep impression on her mind. She saw in her dream that the resurrection morning had come and saw herself rising from the grave to meet her 'glorious redeemer'. The vision was so vivid that she retained the imagery throughout her life. Many years later when she settled down as a married woman at North Tolsta she recognised the place of her resurrection exactly as she had seen it in her dream – 'a green bank decked with a variety of wildflowers, and near which the restless waves spent themselves on a golden strand'. It was here her body would subsequently be laid to rest.

In February 1935 a sudden storm caught several local Tolsta boats at sea. By evening all but two had reached port. Aboard one of the still missing boats was the brother-in-law of Annie Morrison, the lady who recounted this incident. His name was Murdo. Of course, the family were distressed but Margaret assured them that Murdo was safe. He arrived home within an hour of her assurance. However, the other boat was still missing – and on board was Margaret's grandson, another Murdo. Again the family looked to Margaret for assurance – but she remained silent. However, in the early hours of the morning, she suddenly told her daughter-in-law to prepare a meal for her son as she had just received 'a promise from the Lord' that the boat had made it to harbour. And so it proved to be.

Margaret could neither read nor speak English. Neither was there a radio or newspapers in the house. However, on hearing reports of the death of George V in 1936 she predicted that his elder son would never sit on the throne. As we now know Edward abdicated before his coronation. She also expressed concern for a young girl in the Royal family who would, as a result of the succession of George VI, be called on one day to bear a heavy burden – and asked people to pray for her. It was not until 1954, some 25 years later, and long after Margaret's death, that Queen Elizabeth II had this heavy responsibility laid on her shoulders. Margaret MacKenzie died in 1940.

Jessie (Macdonald) MacIver (Bean Aonghais Ruaidh)

Jessie was born in the village of Carloway in 1835. Her father was from Skye and had gone to the Lewis village of Tolsta Cholais as a Schoolmaster.

Jessie, as with all the women we have been examining, possessed the gift of Second Sight or Prophecy. However, she was very careful as to whom she shared her insights with as some mocked her. Nevertheless, her predictions proved accurate. Jessie became well known for predicting which unborn children would become 'servants of the Lord'. One of these predictions related to the youngest of her eight children. When he was born he was named 'Roderick' – but a short time later she returned to the registrar to change the name to 'Samuel' – stating that 'the Lord had given her the name "Samuel" before the child was born' along with the promise that he would become 'a servant of the Lord'. Samuel grew up to be a minister.

Another unborn child she predicted would become a minister was a man who was to become a very well-known minister - Rev. Murdo MacAulay, Carloway. For many years this seemed unlikely as the boy showed no interest in Christianity – but in 1936 he came to faith. Later, having been taken prisoner by German forces during WW2 he started his preaching career in a prisoner of war camp in Germany! The Rev. Norman Macleod of Callanish told a similar story of Jessie in relation to himself.

On one occasion it appeared that Jessie had overstepped herself when she predicted that the unborn child of a friend would also become 'a servant of the Lord'. The baby was a girl – and in these days in Lewis, it was highly unlikely, if not impossible, that she would become a minister! However, the girl, Mary Ann MacDonald later trained to be a nurse and subsequently went to India as a missionary. Jessie died in 1922 almost in her 80th year.

Chirsty Mary Morrison

Chirsty Mary Morrison was born on the 12th of June 1898, in Lingerbay, Isle of Harris. When she was 19 her eyesight began to deteriorate. Although known as 'Blind Chirsty Mary' she was, for most of her life, partially sighted, only fully losing her sight in later years. Chirsty was renowned for speaking her mind, which sometimes resulted in confrontation with the authorities of the Free Presbyterian Church of which she was a member. She had no track with the narrow-mindedness of some within the denomination of her birth and moved freely among Christians of other denominations. This was particularly true at communion times when she would travel far and wide to meet with her fellow believers. Chirsty Mary remained single all her life, living in her own home in Bayhead, Harris, when she was not engaged on some journey!

The distinguishing mark of Chirsty's life, it is said, was prayer. One close friend noted:

> (She) spent much time in prayer and although at times severely tested, her petitions were eventually fulfilled. During such seasons of desertion, when not conscious of the Lord's felt presence, she retired to her room – where she spent hours in prayer, and rocking from side to side in her chair sang a spiritual Gaelic poem mournfully.

Chirsty Mary's journeys became legendary throughout the western Highlands and Islands. Transport in the form of cars, ferries and planes were on many occasions, provided in a miraculous way, when she decided the Lord had instructed her to move on. One morning in Tote on the Isle of Skye, the lady of the house (a friend of the author) in which Chirsty was staying, entered her bedroom to find her on her knees under the blankets, engaged in prayer. A short time later she announced that the Lord had told her she was to return to Harris on the ferry from Uig. However, by that time, the ferry timetable indicated that the ferry had already left. The family in Tote took some persuading but eventually, the man of the house gave in to her pleading and took her the 15 miles to Uig. On arrival, to the man's surprise, the ferry was still at the pier. As soon as Chirsty had reached the top of the gangplank it was raised and the ferry left port.

On another occasion, Chirsty stayed at a home in Stornoway with the intention of catching a flight to Inverness, from where she intended travelling to a communion weekend in Ullapool, a place she had never visited. Flora McNicol, who was a young woman at the time, relates the story:

> It blew a hurricane all through the night, and the following morning. Chirsty Mary insisted that we go to the Airways Office, and book her seat, as she was assured the plane would eventually arrive, after my father had held family worship. He read from the chapter where it was told Philip of the Spirit, 'Go near, and join thyself to this chariot'. This was her confirmation, so we both accompanied her to the Airways Office. On arrival there, the attendant smiled, being acquainted with our passenger and as was as always the case, there was one seat left. I took her to the airport, and some hours later the plane arrived in brilliant sunshine. An hour later I received a telegram worded as follows – 'Chariot met Chariot, till I arrived destination safely, Exceeding joyful, Chirsty Mary.

For some reason, there were those who knew Chirsty but did not always relish her company! After she had become totally blind Chirsty was travelling one day on the ferry between Harris and Skye. On board was a Free Presbyterian minister who thought he would better avoid her (he told the author this story himself) – and sat in a far corner. However, shortly after the boat left Tarbert he heard her calling – 'Mr … is on the boat today. The Lord has told me. Where are you Mr …' The minister crept out of his corner and joined her, stating, as he recounted the incident 'I felt like Adam trying to hide from God in the garden!'

In June 1984, Chirsty Mary was in Bernara, Isle of Lewis for a communion weekend. One evening in the home of some friends someone noticed the colour draining from her face and she became very pale. She was quickly asked if she was all right. She replied that she was, but that two men nearby had just entered eternity. A short time later word reached the home that a local boat had sank and the two men on board had been drowned. Chirsty Mary died in Harris on the 17th May 1989.

ENDNOTE

1. The accounts above relating to women from the Isle of Lewis are drawn from the privatly published booklet - *Christian Women* by the late Annie Morrison. Information in relation to the life of Chirsty Mary Morrison, Harris, comes from personal stories related to and letters received by the author.

CHAPTER 9

Tormod Sona

They are big and learned men over there, but as for myself I have only as the Lord gives me from hour to hour.

Tormod Sona (1852-1945)

One man universally respected in the Isle of Lewis in his day was Norman MacDonald, 'Tormod Sona' (Happy Norman). Born on the island in the spring of 1852 Norman was in touch with a generation who had experienced the storms and birth pains of spiritual awakening throughout Lewis in 1827.

Norman came to faith at the age of 19 and was ordained an elder of Barvas Free Church of Scotland in 1902.

Tormod Sona, as his nickname suggests, was not a morose Christian but maintained a deep joy and lively sense of humour. Marked by a deep spirituality, he was often on his knees. His public prayers by contrast were, it is said, brief and at times even abrupt. His spiritual insight and experience of divine revelation, was, he believed, in answer to prayer. His biographer has noted:

> He could frequently astonish his friends by saying something which showed that hidden things were shown to him. This he had because he had enquired of the Lord of things according to his will relating both to his own life and that of others.[1]

How did Tormod Sona receive the revelations that were to mark his life? Perhaps the easiest way to discover this is to examine some of his experiences.

One night a man in Norman's area was very ill. His wife, a Christian of note, was praying earnestly for her husband's recovery. She asked in her prayer that God would make Norman pray with her. Norman immediately became aware that someone needed his prayers, and was not long on his knees when he found what he referred to as an *"open door"* in the lonely woman's home.

Calling to see her the next day he said, 'You were awake last night, and you would not keep your peace till you had me up also.' A similar event occurred early one morning when Norman found himself unable to sleep with the conviction that someone needed his prayers. In his spirit, he went from door to door village to village, until he found an 'open door' at Europie in Ness. The next time he visited the village he made discrete enquiries, discovering, that on the night in question, a person in the house was very ill.

The following incident also reinforces the way in which Norman was frequently led or impressed.

A woman from North Tolsta, while attending a communion in Shawbost, was passing through a period of spiritual difficulty. Entering a house she found Norman sitting by the fire and after shaking hands with him she quickly left. However, the same evening she found herself in his company once again. Speaking to the gathering Norman said. 'There is someone present who is bearing a great trial, but let me give you this word from the Lord – The Lord upholdeth all that fall, the cast down raiseth up again.' The facts of the matter were that when the woman had entered the house in the morning, these words were 'powerfully presented' to his mind. So much so that he was aware of her burden and compelled to pray for her.

The term used by Norman is interesting - 'Give you this word from the Lord'. This is a clear case of direct revelation of another's need through a powerful impression. Apart from direct 'impression', Norman also received revelation or supernatural knowledge in dreams.

A woman who lived in Canada and was unknown to Norman was passing through 'the deep and troubled waters of spiritual concern.' One night she dreamt that she was standing close to a strange group of people who were praying. A man in the group approached her and placing his hand on her shoulder, spoke kindly to her 'from the scriptures.' In her dream, she felt a sweet peace entering her being, and her trouble giving way to a sense of peace. When she woke the darkness and oppression had passed away.

The woman spoke one day to a friend from Lewis who knew Norman. Describing the man in the dream Norman's friend had no difficulty in identifying him to the woman as Tormod Sona.

Nor was this the only known occasion when Norman's prayers reached well beyond his native shores. On one occasion during the First World War, he told a friend – 'I was in Italy last night, and the German prisons cannot keep my prayers from getting in where the poor prisoners are.' Indeed, a short time before his death, and before it became public knowledge, Norman, accurately informed his son one morning that Hitler had taken his own life.

However real and intimate the revelations Norman MacDonald received, there were naturally times when he did not receive direction. On one occasion when asked by a minister whether or not he had any guidance in relation to a certain matter, he replied, 'There is nothing in the world easier for me to do than to believe God's word; but in this case I have no guidance.'

In the village of South Dell on the Isle of Lewis, there was an elderly Christian lady who Norman held in high regard and with whom he enjoyed 'fellowship in the Spirit.' Meeting her on one occasion she said, 'Did you see the three on whom the dew fell last night? I hope', said Norman, our … was among them.' This elderly lady had received an 'assurance' that God had heard her prayers on behalf of some whose spiritual welfare had been a burden on her spirit.

Someone once commented after hearing Norman preach – 'I never heard anyone preach like you before.' To which he replied, 'Probably not, and you may never hear anyone preaching like this again.' This was not any kind of boast but rather a reference to the fact that he believed few preachers had real spiritual perception. Indeed, so rare was this spirituality becoming, that speaking to a friend one day Norman said, 'I know most of the witnesses in these parts, but there is only one among them who agrees with my own outlook and experience.' This is a telling comment and one that reveals just how far the spirituality of Lewis had sunk since its glory days. Then men and women walked in supernatural revelation, ministers preached in revelation and would break in on their own sermons with 'words of revelation.'

One example of this is recorded of the famed minister known as 'Big MacRae', Rev. John MacRae of Kintail. One Sunday morning Hector Jack, of Strathconon, rose early to go to Knockbain, where MacRae was then minister. As he listened to the preacher, he was astonished to hear his own experiences so accurately described. However, he could not really believe that the preacher was referring to him. At this point, MacRae broke in upon his line of thought and exclaimed,

> Young man, you are wondering if I am referring to
> somebody else, but I am not; I am referring to you who
> were so anxious last night lest you should sleep in, that
> you divested yourself of only part of your clothes when
> you went to bed.

This was exactly what Hector Jack had done, but still he thought
the description might apply to somebody else in the congregation.
Again MacRae raised his voice to a yet higher pitch, and said with
great emphasis,

> You are still thinking young man, that I may be referring
> to someone else in this gathering. To put it beyond all
> doubt for you, I am referring to you, who, in addition
> to what I have already said, prayed beneath the willow-
> bush in your back-garden before you left for Knockbain
> this morning.

Satisfied with this identification the young fellow gratefully
accepted the message as 'from the Lord' and 'with overflowing joy,
gave thanks to God who, by His servant, had spoken to him the
very message that he so urgently needed and desired.'

There is a hint that Norman may have considered an overemphasis
on academic qualities and qualifications as being responsible for
a decline in the revelatory life and preaching. Commenting on
a place a friend had recently visited he said, - 'They are big and
learned men over there, but as for myself I have only as the Lord
gives me from hour to hour'.

Commenting on Norman's experience of revelation the Rev.
Murdoch Campbell, states:

> We see through the bible how the Church, and God's
> people individually, have been guided and preserved in
> all their perils and ways by God's Spirit and Word. They
> sometimes receive spiritual and inward impressions
> which enable them to apprehend where they are and

with whom they are. When Abraham for example, entered Gerar the whole malignant atmosphere of the place reacted on his renewed spirit so much that he exclaimed, "surely the fear of God is not in this place". If similar mystical apprehensions were often present with Norman these we must trace not to any psychological abnormality but to the presence of God's Word and Spirit in his heart. He was a man of such sensitive feelings that he could almost instinctively sense the spirit of other men.

One experience that Norman held in common with many of the seers and mystics of the past, and indeed, some in more modern times, was a supernatural awareness of impending visitors to the house. It is reported that 'he could almost invariably tell his daughter-in-law when any of God's people were about to visit his home'.

On one occasion shortly before a church service, Norman led a small group in worship nearby. As he prayed he forgot about the time. On rising from his knees only one of the company was left, the others having gone on to the service. As Norman and his friend walked to the church, he stopped once more to pray briefly before entering. When the prayer was over he said, 'We may go in. When we shall enter the minister will be in the act of illustrating a portion of the word, and not an eye in the church but will be riveted on his outstretched hand.' And so it proved, no one was distracted as they entered.

Norman had little time for those whose religion consisted of a formal legalism and whose tongue was contrary to their actions. He once said, 'A true Christian could be known even if he had no tongue.'

One night as he was preparing to go to bed a 'word from the Lord' came to Norman. Someone was in need of his help. However, he tried to go to bed obviously thinking that the matter could wait, but to use his own words, 'the one foot refused to follow the other.' He got dressed and went outside. After walking for a considerable distance, praying as he went, he met a person who was in deep distress of body and soul. Norman did all he could to alleviate the situation and help the person in need. Norman MacDonald died in July 1945 aged 93.

ENDNOTE

1. Rev. Murdoch Campbell *The Kings Friend, Memorial of Norman MacDonald or Tormod Sona*, undated, p.7.

CHAPTER 10

Fields of Dreams

I noticed that one of the office-bearers who sat in front of me was extremely agitated, and, in a few seconds, his countenance was changed into the form of our conception of the evil one.

Rev. Peter Chisholm (1884-1957)

One of the fascinating things about the prophetic gift, revelatory dreams or spiritual perception is, as we have seen, that the experience does not appear to be restricted in any way. We find them among the young and old, male and female, religious and irreligious and the educated as well as the uneducated. Peter Chisholm, who was born in Gravir on the Isle of Lewis in 1884 would certainly fall in to the classification of the educated and religious. From what we know of Peter's life his religion was a very narrow one, in fact so narrow that even the most conservative of denominations in Scotland was too liberal for him. Yet he was a Seer - experiencing dreams, impressions and the visualisation of the powers of darkness - even within a 'church' setting.

Coming to faith as a young man, as a result of an intense spiritual and psychological struggle, he subsequently joined the Free Presbyterian Church of Scotland as a student minister. It was while living in Glasgow on a six-month placement in this role that he had one of his early supernatural experiences.

After preaching at St Jude's Free Presbyterian Church, Glasgow, one Sunday evening and while relaxing in the manse, he was 'without any warning, enveloped in a horror of great darkness, accompanied with an unusual, spiritual, depression.' After briefly conducting family worship with the manse family he retired to bed – but he would not find any rest that night. He takes up his own story:

> My mental and physical powers seemed to collapse, all at once. I lay in this semi-comatose condition for over an hour, when, suddenly, several passages of God's Word were brought home to me with sweet persuasiveness. The first was from Isaiah 25. 10-12: "For in this mountain shall the hand of the Lord rest, and Moab shall be trodden down under him, even as straw is trodden down for the dunghill. And he shall spread forth his hands in the midst of them as he that swimmeth spreadeth forth his hands to swim, and he shall bring down their pride together with the spoils of their hands. And the fortress of the high fort of thy walls shall he bring down, lay low, and bring to the ground, even to the dust." The passage which immediately followed was from Matthew 27. 18: "For he knew that for envy they had delivered him." The panorama, which was indelibly fixed on my mind, consisted of the Free Presbyterian Church in its decline and fall. The term "mountain" signifies the proclamation of the Gospel. The "hand of the Lord" refers to the presence of the Holy Spirit, the Third Person of the Godhead, which maketh the reading, but especially the preaching of the Word an effectual means, etc. "Moab," which is trodden down, refers to the enemies of the Lord's heritage. "Their pride" and the "fortress of the high forts" are the religious subterfuges of unregenerate, professing people.

Towards the end of his placement in Glasgow and shortly before returning to Edinburgh where he was living at the time, it fell to him to take a prayer meeting in the same church:

> As it was customary to make a few comments on some passage in the portion read, I waited upon the Lord for some guidance. Later in the day my mind was directed to Achan's transgression (Joshua 7. 1-9). I felt a strong reluctance to meddle with this subject, and, having attempted to choose some other portion, it was strongly impressed upon my mind that I should read the chapter, and make a few remarks on the thoughts presented to my mind, at the time. Having committed my way unto the Lord I proceeded to the meeting. I had some reason for believing all along, that some of the elders were not pulling their weight in my favour. I did not mind that very much, as I was neither an elder's man, nor a minister's man.
>
> After the preliminaries I read the chapter, when I felt that I was more agitated than usual. As I proceeded with the exposition I got a vision – not a dream this time – of what appeared like a black cloud moving slowly above the people from the back of the hall, and coming directly towards me. For a moment I was nonplussed, but it soon became perfectly evident that it was "a messenger of Satan." Realising that it was the aim of the Adversary to confuse my mind, I held on to my subject. Such was the pull in that direction that I was in danger of losing the thread of my discourse. When it had reached my forehead I experience a most unpleasant, suffocating, sensation, but in a second or two my mental equipoise was restored, and I proceeded with my address with composure and liberty. When I came to the point which dealt with the transgression "in the accursed thing" (Joshua 7.1-9) I observed that the New Testament equivalent of the chastisement inflicted is the ordinance of Church discipline, according to the Word of God. I noticed that one of the office-bearers who sat in front of me was extremely agitated, and, in

a few seconds, his countenance was changed into the form of our conception of the evil one.

A short time later he had another dream:

> I dreamed that I was worshipping in St Jude's Church, and the minister was preaching. Although it was only between 12 noon and 1 p.m. the day began to fade away, and soon almost everybody was lulled to sleep, and one could hardly hear the voice of the minister. Suddenly a voice rang out at the main entrance, "Fire." A few rushed into the passages, and soon the commotion became general-rushing and crushing, and trampling one another. As I was among the first to reach the door, I gave a quick glance towards the pulpit, when I saw several men struggling with a long ladder which they had placed against the front of the pulpit. The minister stepped on to the ladder which was then raised almost perpendicular and proceeded to pass out through the roof. At this moment as we were rushing out, the roar of the fire upstairs, and splinters of glass and slates flew all around while the people, wrapping their faces, fled in terror. The import of this vision was fully realised in the breaking up of the congregation into two halves, some years ago.

Chisholm subsequently left the Free Presbyterian Church of Scotland and later became a minister of the Free Church of Scotland. It was while serving in this capacity in Kyle of Lochalsh in 1932 that he again experienced significant dreams. These came at a time when he once more perceived he faced opposition from within his congregation:

> I wrestled at a throne of grace where none pleads in vain – with agonising importunity. Still the hosts of wickedness advanced. I dreamed that they were closing in upon me, whilst I slowly retreated. There were a number of spectators intently awaiting the result. Behind me there stood a stone wall, which would soon bar my way of retreat; and probably bring the contest to

an end. I thereupon, as it were for the last time, scanned the horizon. In doing so what dimly appeared like a bird could be seen very far away. Then I thought it was an angel, and fixing my gaze steadily upon the object, which drew nearer and nearer, I discovered it was a human form standing erect. It stood at my right side, suspended, at some distance from the ground. Such was transcendent brightness with which it was clothed, that, immediately it was directed upon my pursuers, they begun to fade away, until not a shadow of them remained. When I awoke the import of the vision darted into my mind, and is substantially as follows. The party represented by the human visitor had passed way a short time previously. No one knew better who were the enemies and what their designs were, and this was the result of the prayer of faith in her wrestling with the Lord to save her minister. Her prayers were now answered.

As Chisholm had become disenchanted with the Free Presbyterian Church - so also was he now with his current denomination. However, his concerns ran much deeper than that as he was now, apparently, becoming concerned for the very future of Presbyterianism itself. In his book, which is, in part, the title of this chapter, *Wandering in Fields of Dreams,* he records 'Vision 5' as follows:

I was walking along a dyke, inside of which lay the burnt and charred debris of all the Scottish Presbyterian Churches. Arriving at a gap in the dyke, I walked in, and crossed over to a conspicuous monument, some yards away. As I closely examined it, and wondered which Church had stood there, a Free Presbyterian gentleman, carrying an ordinary work man's shovel, came along and spoke to me as follows:- "Although you see our Church, which stood here, burned like the rest, nevertheless, the foundations are perfectly secure, and, if you come along with me, you can verify this for yourself." I followed him across to the dyke, where he began to clear away the ashes and debris, in order to reach the foundation.

After he had digged for a short time, and, as I was looking on, the flames betched out. He walked away and said nothing. Whatever the iniquitous "image of jealousy" may be which rivals Jehovah in his House, and represents the predominating wickedness of the land, it provokes the Holy Spirit that "he should go far off from his sanctuary." The fact of His departure provides the signal for a visitation of wrath. "I will not be with you any more except ye destroy the accursed among you." This was the passage of Scripture by which the Most High warned the present writer of the deterioration of the Free Church, and which considerably agitated his mind for several months before he was informed of the sad state things obtaining to the Church.

His last recorded dream vision appears in a chapter of the book already referred to and is entitled – 'The Return of the Glory':

I was walking along the sea-shore towards some destination further along. The shore consisted of enormous boulders, while the storm was raging with huge billows lashing against the rocks. On the left and in the direction of my objective stood a towering elevation, the face of which was almost perpendicular, beholding which one felt a nasty shudder gripping him. As it was impossible to get along by sea the only alternative was to ascend the cliff. Drawing closer to the foot of the hill, I noticed that a ladder had already been placed against the face of the rock, which extended to the very summit at an enormous height. To climb on that ladder was terrible in the extreme, but it had to be attempted if I were going to reach my destination. What was the nature of the terrain beyond, it was impossible to ascertain. I stepped on to the ladder and began the ascent. When I had gone more than half way I looked back. and saw my brother following me. This increased my trepidation, as I realised that if I lost my hold I should drag him along with me. Cautiously I resolved to carry on as I had not far to go and finally stepped on to terra firma again. The scene which confronted us was entrancing. The sky, sea and land were absolutely calm with bright sunshine and an exhilarating warmth in the air. It was symbolically "new heavens and a new earth, and the former shall not be remembered nor come into mind. But be ye glad and rejoice for ever in that which I create; for behold, I create an new Jerusalem (the universal Church of Christ) a rejoicing, and her people a joy" – the Millennial Church which will now bear 'the glory' and bring healing to the distracted nations of the earth (Isaiah 65:7).

Peter Chisholm died on the 1st of July 1957 aged 77 and is buried in his home village of Gravir on the Isle of Lewis. It is believed he was resident in Broadford, Skye, at the time of his death.

CHAPTER 11

The Reluctant Prophet

I wanted no more of futuristic visions and I prayed that whatsoever was inspiring me into them be taken away from me.

Norman MacLeod (1926-2006)

If there was anyone who, in more recent times, embodied the spirituality and experience of the Seers of a past generation in the Hebrides it was the late Norman MacLeod of Bridge House, Leverburgh, Isle of Harris. Norman, who was born in Leverburgh on the 2nd of March 1926, was a humble and reserved man who, like Chirsty Mary, had been brought up in a very conservative Presbyterian denomination. As was said of James Mathieson, Norman lived on the verge of the natural world and saw far in to the world of spirits.

There is some indication that Norman's mother had, at least in some measure, walked the same path before him. He records the following of her:

During the war our next door neighbour Danny MacRae was with the 8th Army in the Western Desert. One night my mother was dreaming that she saw Danny passing in a closed car and when she attempted to speak to him, he gave a wave as if to tell her that he could not communicate. In the morning she told my father that Danny had been taken prisoner. Shortly afterwards, Tobruck fell to Rommel's forces and Danny's parents received the dreaded telegram that their son was missing. My mother immediately went next door and told the distraught parents of her dream, assuring them that their son was safe and well but a P.O.W. - and so it turned out to be.

What follows is part of Norman's own story, written by him in 2006, shortly before his death.

For more than fifty years, it was clear to me that I was sometimes taken through the bounds of time and getting glimpses of future events. These futuristic visions were mainly in regard to death, tragedies and wars, sometimes in very far away places, often in vague symbolism, invariably in dreams. On other occasions in a seemingly out of body phenomenon, being transported through the future to any part of the world however distant and clearly seeing things as if I was physically present. Not all visions were of impending tragic events. One night I dreamt of being in our back garden, which is backed in one place with steep rocks, mini cliffs in fact, up to ten feet high. With me was a small boy, a mere toddler and I was watching him carefully as he clambered over the rocks. The following morning the phone rang and was answered by my wife, while I continued to prepare the breakfast. She seemed very pleased at the news she was getting over the phone, responding with exclamations such as "isn't that lovely, isn't it wonderful". I wondered what the good news could be, but remembering my dream I shouted, "Tell her it is a boy". Our oldest daughter had been married for several years with no family. I had guessed correctly the news she had for her mother and several months later she did have a boy. There was nothing miraculous of course in guessing correctly when there was only a 50-50 chance of being wrong.

In the year 1963 my father and mother were both staying with us in Skye, while my father was convalescing from what was clearly a terminal illness. He was eighty years of age while my mother at seventy-two seemed hale and hearty. One night I had a dream with scriptural symbolism, I saw the sun and moon low over the horizon moving westward when the moon suddenly turned a very pale colour and slowly sank over the horizon while the sun continued on its course. I refused to accept the obvious interpretation and tried to brush the whole thing out of my mind, but the following night I had the same dream except that this time my father was standing beside me, sorrowfully watching the phenomenon. Then remembering Pharaoh's dream of the coming famine in Egypt, first proclaimed symbolically by the fat and lean kine, the other by the good and poor ears of corn. After interpreting the dream, Joseph concluded that since the dream was repeated to Pharaoh, it was established by God, and would shortly come to pass. So it was with my dream, about a fortnight later my mother was dead. The first indication of her sudden terminal illness was that her face turned the same ashen colour as I saw of the moon.

A few weeks before my mother died, I went to bed as usual in our home in Skye. I did not feel very relaxed so I tried to ease myself into a more comfortable position, only to find that although my mind was wide awake, my body refused to move. I struggled for some time trying to kick-start my nervous system, at first to little avail. Eventually, I seemed to be moving my arms and legs, and after more strenuous effort I felt my head also moving. I still felt that something was wrong and decided to get out of bed in order to sort myself out properly. After standing on the floor, I felt as light as gossamer hopping lightly on the floor. I realised that I had left my body behind me but I did not mind as I had such a wonderful feeling. I hopped lightly on to the windowsill, found myself on the outside of the window. I then simply launched myself into the night floating lightly over the Skye village at a height of about one hundred feet above the houses. After a few moments of enjoying a wonderful feeling, I had a slight lapse of concentration and found myself not over a village in Skye but at the same height over the village of Obbe in Harris. I continued to glide slowly until I found myself over a small loch in the middle of the village. I hovered over the loch while I took in the view. To my amazement I saw that that the whole village was in darkness except my parents' house where every window was lit up. I then glided down and alighted on to the road in front of the house. I had a look around from that perspective and found that it was no illusion; every house in the village was in darkness except my parents' house, which was all lit up. As I tried to reason why this should be, I woke up in my bed in Skye. A few weeks later a bus I was travelling in along with some friends and the mortal remains of my mother rounded a bend, which took us into view of my parent's house. I found it exactly as I saw it a few weeks previously in my prophetic dream or whatever. Every house in the village was in darkness, except my parent's house which was all lit up. Kind neighbours having opened the house, lit fires and aired beds etc. in preparation of my arrival with my mother's remains.

One night in the spring of 1982, I went to bed pleasantly tired. I just lay on my back gazing at the ceiling, when I found myself not looking at the dark ceiling but at a lovely sun-lit blue sky interspersed with white clouds. It all seemed quite natural, until the sky suddenly swallowed me or that I simply fell into it. A couple of seconds later, whatever was propelling me left me stranded about 150 miles above the earth, whatever gave me that estimate, I do not know. Abandoned in outer space completely disorientated, threshing around trying to find some cohesion with no sense of up, down or direction. I shouted, probably a prayer. I must have been dreaming I explained to my rudely awakened wife, on finding myself wide-awake in bed beside her. On the following two nights, I dreamt of being in a house where psalms were being sung. Connecting the two experiences together, I concluded that a man of God would soon be snatched to Glory so suddenly that he would know nothing about it until he found himself there. About a fortnight later a Godly missionary, an Elder in the FP Church dropped off his feet in a sheep fank, dead. I am convinced, he entered glory before his empty shell of a body struck the ground.

In the late nineteen fifties or early sixties, before I had ever seen news on the television, I dreamt that I was seeing a full moon in the sky but as I continued to look it became apparent that it was not the moon I was seeing but a globe of the earth spinning on its axis, with the continents and nations clearly shown, As I continued to look my attention was drawn to the South East corner of Asia, Vietnam, which until then did not spell war. Then as I watched I saw a huge intercontinental rocket being fired from there straight into the sky leaving a massive trail of smoke. So ended the vision, but some months or perhaps years later when I first saw news on T.V. I recognised the spinning earth globe prelude on the screen as identical to what I had seen in the dream vision several months earlier. Not long after I first had access to news on television, the American involvement in the Vietnamese war was the main news.

Another time, I saw a war in central Africa with two North African Muslim nations taking opposing sides. That actually happened in the Congo or whatever that nation was called at the time. This was probably in the middle of the nineteen sixties.

On another occasion, I saw a war in the Balkans. A mountainous part of it, probably Albania, with street fighting and men shooting at each other from behind cars.

Another time in the year 1982 I dreamt of being over Israel and Lebanon in some sort of aeroplane. A war was on there at the time. On looking I saw what I took to be a new moon in the sky but someone I did not see said over my left shoulder "it is not a new moon but a new earth". I took it from that, not to expect peace in that part of the world until the Prince of Peace himself came to establish a new earth.

Another time in the early eighties I saw a deep trench running north to south in the middle-east, through Iraq or on the border with Iran with a fire blazing the whole length of it. Later I took this to be the Iran-Iraq war, which lasted 8 years and possibly extended to the current era.

Falklands War

One night in the spring of 1982 one word kept drumming all night into my head, Falkland, Falkland, not Falkland Islands or even Falklands. The only Falkland I could think of was a small town in Fife, which made no sense to me. However, about a fortnight later things became clearer with the Argentinean invasion of South Georgia, followed by the actual invasion of the Falkland Islands. From then on I could just about write the whole history of that war, as days to more than a week in advance, night after night I was given a very clear picture of what would happen.

At first the war was a bloodless one, but one night I saw a crowd of men trapped in a sunken ship, with a submarine involved. I first took it to be one of the British nuclear submarines becoming a casualty. It transpired however that one of our submarines sank the Argentinean battleship, the General Belgrano. On another occasion I saw a battleship with its metal superstructure on fire, white incandescent flames leaping high into the sky. I could not understand how the steel superstructure of a battleship could burst into flames but when the news eventually caught up with the vision, a few days later, it transpired that the superstructure of the flaming battleship, HMS Sheffield, was made of aluminium, and not steel. Aluminium is very combustible under intense heat. What eventually appeared on television was exactly as I had seen previously in my sleep in Harris.

Another night I could not get to sleep, for as soon as my head touched the pillow, I had visions of blood and fire. It continued into the following day, even when I dropped off to sleep in the fireside chair. Visions included seeing a fair-haired young man horribly injured on the side of his face and head. Three or four days later the troop ship, Sir Galahad, carrying Welsh Guards was struck by guided missiles causing heavy casualties, horrible injuries and severe burns.

I have forgotten most of the visions I saw during this war but there is one experience I can never forget. I found myself standing on a moor on the Falkland Islands, not unlike the Lewis moor, fairly level, the sky was overcast, it was neither dark nor very light, like dawn or late evening. Open in front of me was a deep, wide trench. Along the side of the trench were bodies wrapped in off-white fabric and they were being handed down to men in the trench. Someone spoke to me over my left shoulder and told me that they were being buried and among them was a high-ranking person. Some days later the Marines attacked Goose Green, sustaining heavy casualties, among whom was their commanding officer Colonel H Jones, the highest ranking British officer killed in that war. Later the dead were temporarily buried in canvas coffins, later to be raised and taken home for burial. When the picture of the burial appeared sometime later on television I could see that it was exactly as I had seen it in a dream, or more likely an out of body experience 8000 miles away from home.

I was very much against going to war over the sovereignty of the Falkland Islands. The Falkland Islands and all

1200 inhabitants had been forgotten, abandoned and completely neglected by the British Government. I had no doubt that they would be far better off under Argentinean rule. I reckoned by ordinary common sense that the war would cost the life of one serviceman and £1,000 000 for every man, woman and child on the islands. As far as human life was concerned I could not have been closer but I do not believe that I reached 10% of the fiscal cost of the war. Margaret Thatcher's reputation as the 'iron lady' had to be protected, regardless of casualties.

As the war was nearing its end, with British troops having advanced to the outskirts of Port Stanley, news coming over the television was warning to expect impending casualties, as the Argentinean forces were expected to make a desperate last stand. I felt very depressed over this and my wife who was in and out of the kitchen was actually in tears. Then I nodded off to sleep and instantaneously found myself sitting on a low hillside above the harbour of Port Stanley. I could see ships anchored over a wide area of the sea and one ship seemed to have been hit by a bomb or missile. I seemed to zoom in on it and saw sailors clearing the debris, dumping some in the sea. None of them seemed in any way disturbed. I looked all around me and at the sky. It was heavily clouded as I always saw it over the Falklands but as I looked up, the clouds rolled back from directly above me revealing a single bright star. I then woke up in my fireside chair at home, having been absent for no more that a few seconds but in that time I nipped out to the war zone one third around the earth's circumference, got an accurate account of the war a couple of days in advance, and was back before my wife noticed a drop in our conversation. I said to her "don't worry, there will be no more killing, the war is over". Then added a slight correction, "one ship will still be struck by one bomb, near its stern, but no life will be lost". And so it was, to the very last detail.

9/11 Terror attack on New York

My most fearful dream vision came to me about three weeks before the 9/11 terror attack on New York. I found myself standing at a window of a high building when an atomic bomb went off about half a mile away. I covered my eyes with my hands to protect them from the brighter-than-the-sun flash of light that I knew would follow. That did not help however, so I folded my arms over my eyes but the overpowering light still got through. I then curled myself up in the foetal position on the floor typical of when a person is being burnt to death. The fearful light nevertheless seemed to penetrate to the very core of my being.

Admittedly it was not a very accurate picture of what actually happened in New York but on the other hand a nuclear explosion was probably the best way of conveying to my mind the sheer horror of what was experienced by the occupants of the twin towers as the aircraft crashed into them. Why I should have been given a distorted picture of the 9/11 horror, I have no idea. It left me with insufficient data to warn anyone of the impending disaster. There was one thing, however that did not deviate from reality and that was the sheer horror of the experience. On waking up in terror, it took me several minutes to convince myself that I was still alive, although I was in no doubt that something terrible was going to happen.

It was about this time that I decided that I wanted no more of futuristic visions and I prayed that whatsoever inspiring me into them be taken away from me. I soon realised that like Jonah, I had taken the coward's way out. Never was prayer marked with a more positive response. Visions of the future simply ceased, much to my regret. I have since seen nothing of portended world events and practically nothing of happenings nearer home.

Conclusion

Gifts of the Spirit are enumerated by the Apostle Paul in his 12th and 14th chapters of first Corinthians as healing, tongues; miracles; prophecy etc. In the increasingly materialistic, long established Western Churches, it is invariably accepted that such supernatural phenomenon did not outlast the Apostolic age. Not so to this day in more recently established churches in developing countries such as China, Nigeria and Islamic countries where Christianity is being persecuted, where the Gospel seed falls on fallow but fertile ground. There miracles of healing still occur and the dead are on occasions raised to life. Quite unacceptable in the West but there is plenty of evidence that it does take place.

Prophecy is rather more difficult to define or prove than other Gifts and is possibly less necessary. The Prophet Amos states "A lion roars who will not fear. The Lord God has spoken who can but prophesy" – almost declaring that with the word of God available in the Bible, it is almost impossible for anyone not to prophecy! Job appears to see prophecy as an ongoing occurrence. "Why, seeing times are not hid from the Almighty do they that know him not see his day." (Job 24 v 1).

Western churches invariably define prophecy as forth telling rather than foretelling, so why not leave it at that. One particular reason is that prophecy is a means by which God proves that he is God (Isaiah Chs. 43 and 46). An assumption by atheists that it is impossible for God or man to see the future until it happens would need to be refuted by any evidence available to the contrary. Hence the reason that I am throwing my Widow's mite of evidence into the balances. Being an ardent Christian believer of very near four score years and fully believing that soon I will have to stand before the judgement seat of Christ, am I likely to jeopardise my eternity on a bit of cheap sensationalism if I was not in deadly earnest.

I know that what I have written, briefly, laboriously with shaky and badly aimed fingers on an unfamiliar computer, itself one of the myriad symbols of the last days which now beset us on every side, will bring much scorn and derision on my grey head. Nevertheless, being in my eightieth year, a cancer survivor, suffering from diabetes and recently a heart attack, aware that the grim reaper must be snapping at my heels, I feel compelled to come into the open, in case the sin of burying my solitary talent in the ground along with myself, will be laid to my account at the Great Assize.

Norman MacLeod
An T-Ob
Isle Of Harris

In addition to his own experiences recorded above Norman also shared the following stories in relation to his home island:

Margaret MacDonald - Strond

In 1875 four young men from Strond in Harris (mere teenagers) set off in the month of February on a most foolhardy fishing expedition to tiny islands 10 miles into the Atlantic. Their boat was a 20 foot sailing skiff. A blizzard of snow and an easterly gale overtook them and to keep their small vessel afloat they had to sail with shortened sail with the wind. They were eventually blown about 100 miles into the Atlantic losing sight of St Kilda. By the grace of God and skilful boatmanship they managed to stay afloat until the wind slackened and changed. Three days after they left Strond they made landfall in Valtos, Uig, Lewis where they were hospitably received and nursed beck to fitness, but it was several days afterwards before news of their safety reached Strond and 11 days from they sailed from Strond before they returned. Their families in Strond (very much a praying village at that time) were not left in darkness. A Godly Strond lady, Margaret MacDonald, married name Ross, living in Finsbay was on her Knees praying, her soul burdened with the seeming tragedy when the words of Psalm 107: 29-39 (He maketh the storm a calm, so that the waves thereof are still. Then are they glad because they be quiet; so he bringeth them unto their desired haven.) spoke so clearly to her, that she threw a cloak or plaid over her shoulders and walked the 6 or 7 miles to Strond with the good news that the lads were safe and well.

Catherine Ferguson - Taransy

Catherine Ferguson, from the Island of Taransy (of Castaway fame) a Godly woman of Heavenly visions had three sons in the first World War. One of them Ronald was a regular soldier, a veteran of many bloody engagements before that war. Catherine said with strong conviction that they would all return safely. Ronald in particular was on the face of battle throughout the war in the Flanders trenches, escaping death on innumerable occasions. On one particular occasion his kilt was reduced to fragments about his legs, but he escaped without a scratch.

Norman Paterson - Strond

Before dawn, Norman Paterson of Strond woke up his fishermen sons and asked them to ferry him over the treacherous ten mile wide Sound of Harris to North Uist, explaining that a brother in Christ living on the Monach Isles seventeen miles off the east side of Uist was in deep soul distress and needing his help. Refusals and excuses were brushed aside and finally his sons took him over the turbulent waters of the Sound of Harris to the nearest point on North Uist. From there he walked about fifteen miles to a point on the west side of Uist where he hoped to hitch a lift on one of the fishing boats operating in the region of the Monachs. He stayed the night with some friends but before he retired he arranged with a fisherman to take him to the Monachs, who asked him to be on the shore at 8 am on the following morning. The people he stayed with asked him not to trust the man but to be on the shore at least an hour earlier but he would not agree and turned up at 8 am as arranged, only to see the boat hull down on the horizon. They will be back he assured his friends. No sooner had he said that that the boat turned back. They had forgotten to take their bait container from the shore.

Da-riridh – Glenurquhart

Around 1900, a Godly man from Glenurquhart, known as Da-riridh ("yes indeed or definitely" – a remark he often made, his mainland Gaelic sounding slightly unusual to Harris ears) lived in Harris. He was very much an itinerant, attending all the places of worship and especially communions. In the main, he lived in Northton but when away from home he was never refused a night's shelter. That is except on one occasion when a surly individual living in an isolated place turned him away from his door. When that inhospitable individual died many years later and was buried in Luskentyre cemetery, the grass did not grow on his grave. His relatives often put fresh turf on the grave but the only effect that had was that the red scar of dead grass was so large that it could be seen about two miles away. Da-riridh was a man in constant prayer and seemingly in constant communication with the Heavenlies.

On one occasion some young lads saw him kneeling behind a dyke and crept up to listen. Da-riridh seemed to be more in conversation than in the usual type of prayer, asking questions and appearing to receive answers.

Da-riridh was the first ever recorded hitch hiker in Harris! Having left Tarbert to walk the seventeen miles to Northton, he was overtaken by the post gig and asked for a lift. The postman declined, saying it would be too much for the pony. At that time in Harris, a pony and gig was by far the fastest form of transport but when the postman arrived in Northton, not having gone off the road, the first man that met him was Da-riridh. To the inevitable question, 'How on earth did you get here?', Da-riridh replied, 'The chariots of God are twenty thousand, thousands of mighty angels.'

On yet another occasion at a communion held in the open air, there being too large a congregation for the church building to hold, Da-riridh was seen to leave his place on the hillside, walk to the edge of the congregation, look around and return to his place. After the service, someone remarked to him on the size of the congregation. 'You should have seen the crowd round about was his reply.' What crowd Da-riridh was referring to is not known but those who knew the man believed it was an angelic host such as surrounded Elisha at Samaria, 2 Kings, Ch. 6, 'The Angels of the Lord encampeth about them that fear him.'

One day, on the Machair at Seilebost (Harris), he stuck his stick into the ground and declared, "A church will stand on this spot yet." A very unlikely prediction at that time, the whole west side of Harris having been cleared of its people some eighty years before that. Nevertheless, some years after the first World War, the area was again divided into crofts and a church was built. Now with the fragmentation of the church, two congregations worship there within yards of each other.

We end this chapter with another, earlier, story from Norman's pen. It relates, not to Second Sight, but to a miraculous and well-documented event witnessed and recounted to him by his father. The minister referred to in this story was the Rev. Ewen MacQueen, who was born on the 17th of June 1866, in Camustinavaig, Braes, Isle of Skye.

Interestingly, MacQueen himself had come to faith as the result of experiencing 'a heavenly vision of effulgent splendour' when, as a young man walking near Sligichan in Skye, 'the heavens opened before him'. He went on to be a highly respected minister, not only within his own denomination but much further afield. By all accounts, he was a humble, loving man.[1]

Under The Shadow of The Almighty

Appeliating a meteorological phenomenon by person's name did not start in the Caribbean. The people of Obbe, Harris, pandering to the desire of Lord Leverhulme to have his name perpetuated in the fishing town he hoped to build, went the second mile with him, naming not only their village after him but also a hurricane that went some way to demolishing it on 20th March, 1922.

In the brief half hour it lasted "Geala mor Libhear" (Hurricane Lever) created unbelievable havoc. Many of Leverhhume's partly constructed buildings were levelled as if by a sythe; a fourteen foot rowing boat turned upside down on the ground for painting simply vanished without trace, as if swallowed whole by the elements, but, that leads to our tale, it blew the roof off the Free Presbyterian Church in Finsbay.

The following August, when the Sacrament of the Lord's Supper fell due to be celebrated in Finsbay, there being no church building, the congregation assembled on the open ground. A small square, ox shaped portable hut serving as a pulpit and white cloth covered benches as the communion table were set at the foot of a slope on which the congregation, numbering about four hundred people, sat on the ground. Included in the congregation were people from other church denominations who also were heard to relate the following account.

The Free Presbyterian minister in Harris at the time was the Reverend Donald T. MacLeod[2] and assisting him at the communion was the Reverend Ewan MacQueen, a preacher of Godly fervour and eloquence, much respected in Harris and elsewhere.

In the morning, the weather was any anything but promising. Dark clouds, thickening lowering and menacing, rolling in on a freshening southerly wind betokening a day of rain, like enemy forces determined to deprive the little flock assembled on the Finsbay Hillside of the soul nourishing celestial dew they were anticipating.

Finally the lowering clouds caught the top of Roneval, (a nearby hill that has of late even acquiring nationwide fame) a portend to those familiar with local weather conditions of an imminent downpour of rain.

The service nevertheless commenced in the usual manner with Mr. MacQueen reading a portion of a Psalm and asking it to be sung. No sooner had the singing started however than the first drops of threatened rain made their arrival and in a futile bid to avoid a drenching, women began opening umbrellas here and there over the hillside.

Mr MacQueen was then seen to stand up in the pulpit box and look around rather impatiently at the gathering storm. He could read the signs of the skies as well as anyone there and well understood that it was no passing shower he was seeing but the start of heavy continuous widespread rain that no power on earth could stop. Ewan MacQueen, however knew of One who is "Mightier than the noise of many waters", and even if nothing short of a miracle from his hand could save the situation, like the good shepherd he was, faithful to his Master and mindful of the vulnerable flock in his charge, the seeming hopelessness of the situation did not deter him from asking for and expecting even that.

Mr. MacQueen stooped down, tapped the presentor on the shoulder to put a sudden stop to the singing: "We will say a word of prayer before we go any further" he announced. With that, he prayed fervently, with all the ardour in his heart and soul and what was described as an almost frightening boldness, specifically for the Lord to stop the rain to enable them to perform the duty they had embarked upon.

The writer can recall some of the exact words used, as told by his father who was present. Translated from Gaelic to the best of his ability as is the whole of this account, they read; "If the rain must fall, there are plenty of villages round about on which that can happen, and if people should happen to be worshipping as we are, they have houses over their heads but we have only the open field." A lady from Geocrab, still hale and hearty, recalls the prayer she heard as a twelve year old; "He implored the Lord fervently and with a boldness that was frightening, that he would put a stop to the rain".

It was clear to all present that Mr MacQueen's faith was absolute and that he considered that he had every right in the circumstances to a favourable response from the Lord. No one seemed able to recall if the will of the Lord was taken into account.

He will fulfill the desire of them that fear him. He will also hear their cry.

God who heard in Heaven gave his reply, immediately, mightily and miraculously. The rain stopped, umbrellas were folded, the Psalm singing resumed and the rest of the Communion service continued in the usual solemn and unhurried manner. Throughout the four hours that the service lasted, not a drop of rain fell on the Communion site. That did not mean that there was any general alteration in the weather. The skies remained as dark and foreboding as ever, rain could be seen falling at not too far a distance all around. The clouds did not lift from the top of Roneval and amazingly tiny rivulets on the steep north face of the hill were soon cascading white and swollen as if by a heavy downpour of rain.

In those days, most of the men present were seamen, fishermen and crofter, people whose livelihood and on occasions their very lives depended on their skill in predicting the weather. They well understood that it was nothing natural they were witnessing, that it was no passing summer shower that was falling around them but a continuous downpour that should not have left a dry spot throughout the whole North West of Scotland. Nowadays it would have been given the meteorological identity of a vigorous rain laden low-pressure area streaming in from the Atlantic.

This was fully proven to people from surrounding villages when they returned home that evening to families who expected them to be drenched.

Although the man made church building of stone and lime succumbed to the wind, following the 'effectual fervent prayer of a righteous man', the real church, the assembly of believers, was permitted to pursue its worship and fulfil its obligation in regard to the sacrament of the Lord's Supper on an exposed hillside in the midst of a rain-storm, as dry and comfortable and in enfolded in the 'Secret of the Lord's Pavilion', which undoubtedly it was.

No information has survived of individual conversions following the various services at this memorable Communion Season, but as evidence that a great cloud of witnesses were fully convinced that "the effectual fervent prayer of a righteous man availeth much", this story has been repeatedly told around many a hearth in Harris for scores of years and there are some alive to this day (2002) who can recall in awe that they were witnesses to the rebuke of the Almighty leaving the communion hill at Finsbay as dry as Gideon's fleece while the whole country side in every direction was drenched. As if the Lamb of God had thrown a corner of his vesture in love and compassion over his beloved.

ENDNOTES

1. Ewen MacQueen was the fourth son of Alexander MacQueen, a crofter shoemaker, who had a family of six sons and one daughter.

After completing his Theological training at Wick, Ewen was ordained and inducted as the first minister of the Free Presbyterian Church in Tarbert, Harris, in 1900. In November 1902, he married Miss Jessie Campbell of Glenvarigill, Skye. The marriage took place in Glasgow, the ceremony being performed by Prof. J. R. Mackay D.D. (1865-1939), then FP minister in Inverness.

It is said Ewen MacQueen's preaching was 'for the most part experimental (his) style of oratory held his audiences spellbound.' In other words, he appealed to the heart and experience – not only to the head. He also visited Canada and America as deputy of the Free Presbyterian Church on three occasions.

It is also reported that:

> 'During communion seasons, crowds flocked to hear the Word of God from his mouth. Men, women and children of all denominations loved him. In the town of Inverness, he was known and respected by almost everybody. He was noted for his attendance at sickbeds in homes and hospitals. Nor did he confine his visits to members of his own congregation. When visiting a hospital, he first made a round of all the beds and usually concluded with public prayer standing in the middle of the ward. Many patients were blessed and greatly encouraged by his earnest prayer and looked forward eagerly to his regular visitations.'

Ewen MacQueen preached his last sermon 'with great liberty from Zechariah chap. 12, verse 10, at a prayer-meeting on November, 9th, 1949.' He died two weeks later in Raigmore Hospital, Inverness. It is said the 'last words on his lips, (were) peace, peace.'

2. There appears to be a typographic error in Norman's document here. The minister he refers to was one Donald Norman MacLeod not Donald T Macleod. Donald Norman MacLeod (1872-1967) was born 29th September 1872, at Eval, North Uist. He died on the 5th of April 1967 and is buried at Morefield Cemetery, Ullapool.

Norman MacLeod was a personal friend of the author and this book is dedicated to his memory. As stated earlier, Norman was born in 1926. He joined Inverness-Shire Constabulary (later Northern Constabulary) as a Police Officer in 1949. He was promoted to Detective Sergeant in 1971 - a post in which he was highly regarded both by his colleagues and the public alike.

A now-retired Police Superintendent who shares the same name and who knew Norman well wrote the following tribute:

Norman was a legend in the Inverness-Shire Constabulary which I joined as a Cadet in 1966. As a young Constable, he was very fit and strong and used to compete in the Police sports day in all heavy events such as the hammer and shot putt. He was a keen mountaineer and active in the (Lochaber) Mountain Rescue Team. He knew Ben Nevis like the back of his hand. He was a determined, dogged character who always had a smile on his face. He understood the public and knew how to handle all sorts in society. Norman was very highly regarded by the general public. He was a strict Free Presbyterian by faith and was the most unassuming character. He never boasted about anything and was a reserved individual but when put to the test in the witness box could hold his own with any defence lawyer. Norman was a true gentleman, an excellent colleague and a godly man who was a pillar in society.

Like many in his culture, Norman was never quite sure about the gift he so clearly exhibited. Speaking of his experience as a younger man, he noted of the prophetic gift - 'I make no claim to such, nor was I presumptuous enough to ascribe any experience I had with the Holy Spirit. Rather putting it down to a mild form of 2nd sight which I was very cautious of.'

However, he would later write, 'Some visions undoubtedly had the signature of the Holy Spirit all over them with scriptural symbolism.' He goes on:

My experiences invariably touched on things of the future, ranging from things a few minutes into the future to about 20 years. Almost invariably it was in dream vision that the veil of the future was drawn back. Such dreams differed from the usual nonsense, in that the visions were very real and vivid, as was my presence there often knowing that I was dreaming. Always it was neither light nor dark but like the grey light of dawn.

As we have already noted the time came when Norman prayed that the gift would cease - it did, immediately, and to his later disappointment, irrevocably. Norman died in Harris on Saturday the 4th of November, 2006.

CHAPTER 12

Thoughts & Considerations

All that we have been considering raises a number of questions. How do we account for the impressions, premonitions, prophecies, visions or dream revelations we have been examining here? Do they still manifest themselves today - and if not why not? If they do, why do we not, in our connected age, hear more about them? Is the source of such phenomena from a spiritual realm or from some more natural, innate, perhaps mostly untapped, gift that is available to all? If the source is spiritual or supernatural does the revelation, vision, etc., originate in a mystical/spiritual realm which is innocuous or from either a good or evil source - or perhaps both?

Before we consider some of these questions I think there are more mundane reasons, in our own day and generation, as to why such phenomena appears to have become much rarer than it once was. First of all our forefathers lived at a time long before all of the distractions that are available to us today - television, instant communication and continual noise, to name but a few. In addition, they did not have the availability of quick and easy travel or luxury accommodation and central heating - the latter which drives the members of a family today into the seclusion of their own rooms along with their personal gadgets of communication. In other words, they lived, in general, in a quieter, slower, sedate and more communal age. In addition, and of necessity, they lived much closer to nature and the natural rhythms of life. In all of that, they had more time and space to communicate with nature, the spiritual world and with one another.

Another reason is the move away from the acceptance of the mystical and spiritual to a rationalistic worldview - a world where everything is subservient to reason and rational explanation. This happened, it appears to me, at its most deadly level in the world of religion - where, once accepted, experiences of the mystical and the prophetic, were abandoned to the philosophies of rationalistic theologians and thinkers. As we have noted there is a hint of this in Tormod Sona's comment - 'They are big and learned men over there, but as for myself I have only as the Lord gives me from hour to hour.' But this is also true of society in general - and it is not without significance that the world of the mystical and the mystic lasted longest in the more remote parts of the Highlands and Islands that we have been examining here.

As we have seen, the writers we have focused on in this book were at pains to try and prove the validity of the mystical visions, impressions and revelations they have recounted - particularly in relation to their religious peers and colleagues who opposed them. And yet opposition from with the religious community, as is the case even today, especially among conservative evangelicals, highlights a great problem. As far as I am aware, the theology of such groups precludes attributing 'omniscience' (the state of knowing everything) to the devil or the powers of darkness. One such group states quite categorically - 'The devil is not, nor can he be, omniscient. If he were omniscient, he would be God.' Of course, this raises the question - how can the devil or the powers of darkness be the source of prophetic visions, futuristic dreams, impressions or premonitions if such is denied to them? And yet some would go so far as to suggest such to be the case. But, as I have said, they face an insurmountable theological problem - a problem I have never heard satisfactorily addressed.

So we are left with the two other propositions- that there is either a natural explanation that can account for such phenomena or that the source is an Omniscient, Omnipresent, Spiritual Being and/or His agents who communicate at a mystical, spiritual level with humanity by means of visions, dreams, premonitions, impressions or direct revelations.

As to those who have experienced these things we also have, ultimately, two possibilities - they are either lying (perhaps deluded) or truthful. As a person who has interviewed countless witnesses over a 30-year career in law enforcement - I have come to the conclusion that it is beyond the realms of credibility not to believe that most, if not all, of the instances recorded here, are truthful. In addition, I have experienced some of them personally and known others of impeccable character and honesty who have also.

That such revelations still exist in our societies in general I have no doubt whatsoever. That they do not, to the extent outlined in this book, is also undeniable, the reasons for which, at least in part, we have suggested above.

I believe we live in a day when, in general terms, as I have already suggested, the rationalistic worldview which exists and has existed for a very long time now, in our society at large and has also, to a greater or lessor extent, been imbibed by traditional religion, has totally failed us. We desperately need a return to the mystical – the spiritual – where The Omniscient One is allowed, once again, to interact with His Creation. Who knows what might happen if we do?

Since this is a book of stories it is only appropriate that we end with one. And it is one where the truly unexpected did in fact happen.

In his book *Island Spirituality* (2013), Alastair McIntosh recounts a very interesting personal story in relation Torcuil MacRath, the late 'Bard of Grimshader', on the Isle of Lewis. Visiting him one day when he was in his 80s Torcuil greeted Alastair enthusiastically. Alastair, whose father had been a local doctor, takes up the account:

> "I am very glad that you have come, a bhalaich," (boy) he said, in a tone of unusual urgency, as I stepped through his door on a visit back to North Lochs. "You see," he said, moving straight to the point, sitting me down in the chair that he always emphasised had belonged to his grandmother. "Since I last saw you, I have seen an angel. At least, it must have been an angel, because I do not know what else it could have been." He pulled his chair right up against mine, coming so close that it was hard to focus. "You see, a bhalaich – I used to have a disease. Your father knew all about it. He had tried everything to treat it, but even to himself, this disease was incurable. Then one day since I last saw you, in the middle of the night, I woke up. And there was this – figure – standing at the foot of my bed. As real as you're sitting there. A presence. Just like a person." "Were you afraid?" I asked, after a long pause. "O, no fear, a bhalaich! No fear! I was not afraid! I just knew, beyond any doubt, that from then on my disease was cured. And that is how it was."

L - #0089 - 030823 - C0 - 216/140/7 - PB - DID3648018